My name is

....

My teacher's name is

....

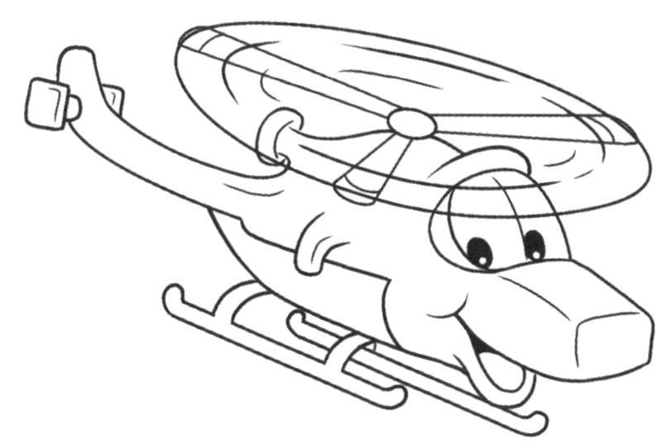

My learning goals and success criteria:

- I can trace and write all lower-case letters of the alphabet.
- I can trace and write all capital letters of the alphabet.
- I can trace and write the numerals 1 to 100.

Are you ready to write?

Posture

Is your back resting against the chair?

Are your feet flat on the floor?

Paper position

left-handed

Are you holding the paper steady with your non-writing hand?

right-handed

Pencil grip

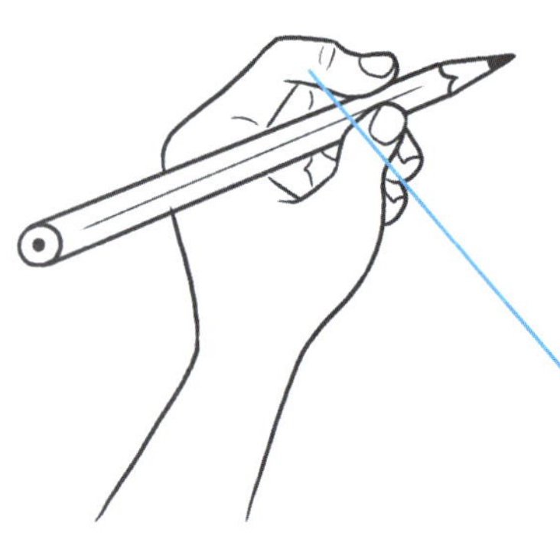

Is one finger on top of the pencil?

Left-handers, hold your pencil a little further up so you can see your handwriting!

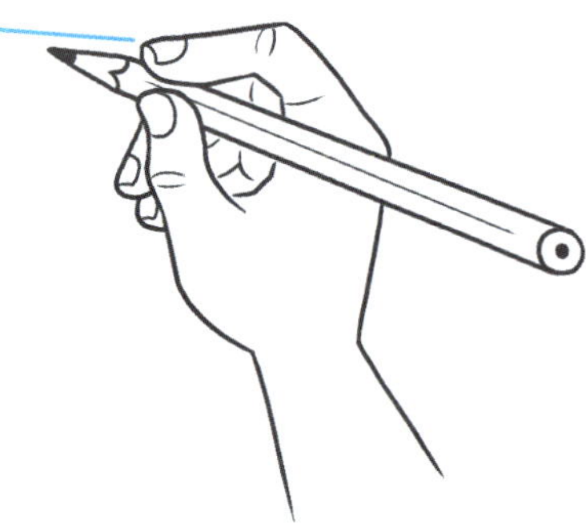

1, 2, 3, 4! Are my feet flat on the floor?
5, 6, 7, 8! Is my back up nice and straight?
9, 10, 11, 12! Show me how your pencil's held!
Thumb and pointer side-by-side, lucky tall one takes a ride!

Start at the dots. Follow the arrows.

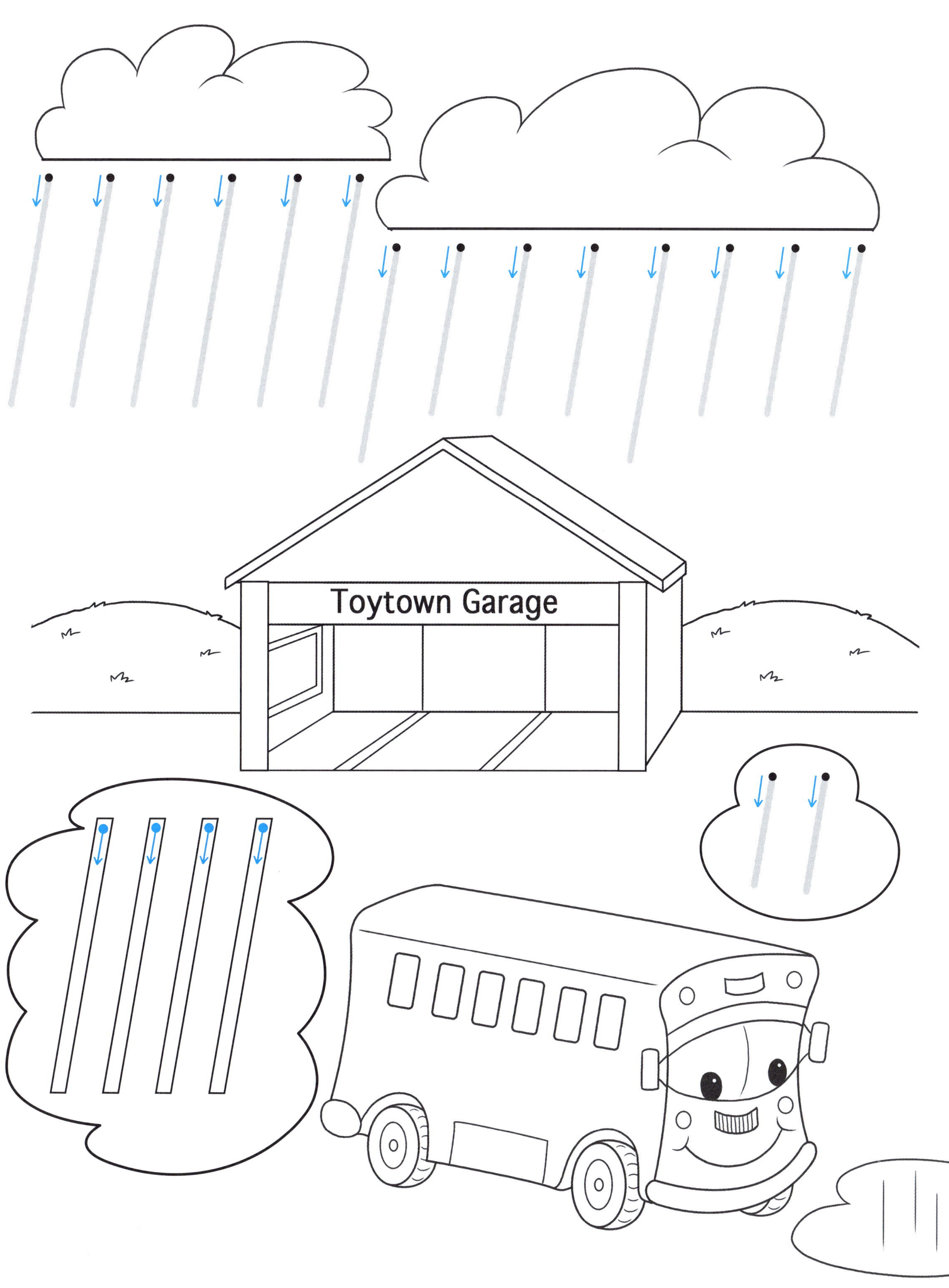

Start at the dots. Follow the arrows.

Start at the dots. Follow the arrows.

Start at the dots. Follow the arrows.

Start at the dots. Follow the arrows.

Start at the dots. Follow the arrows.

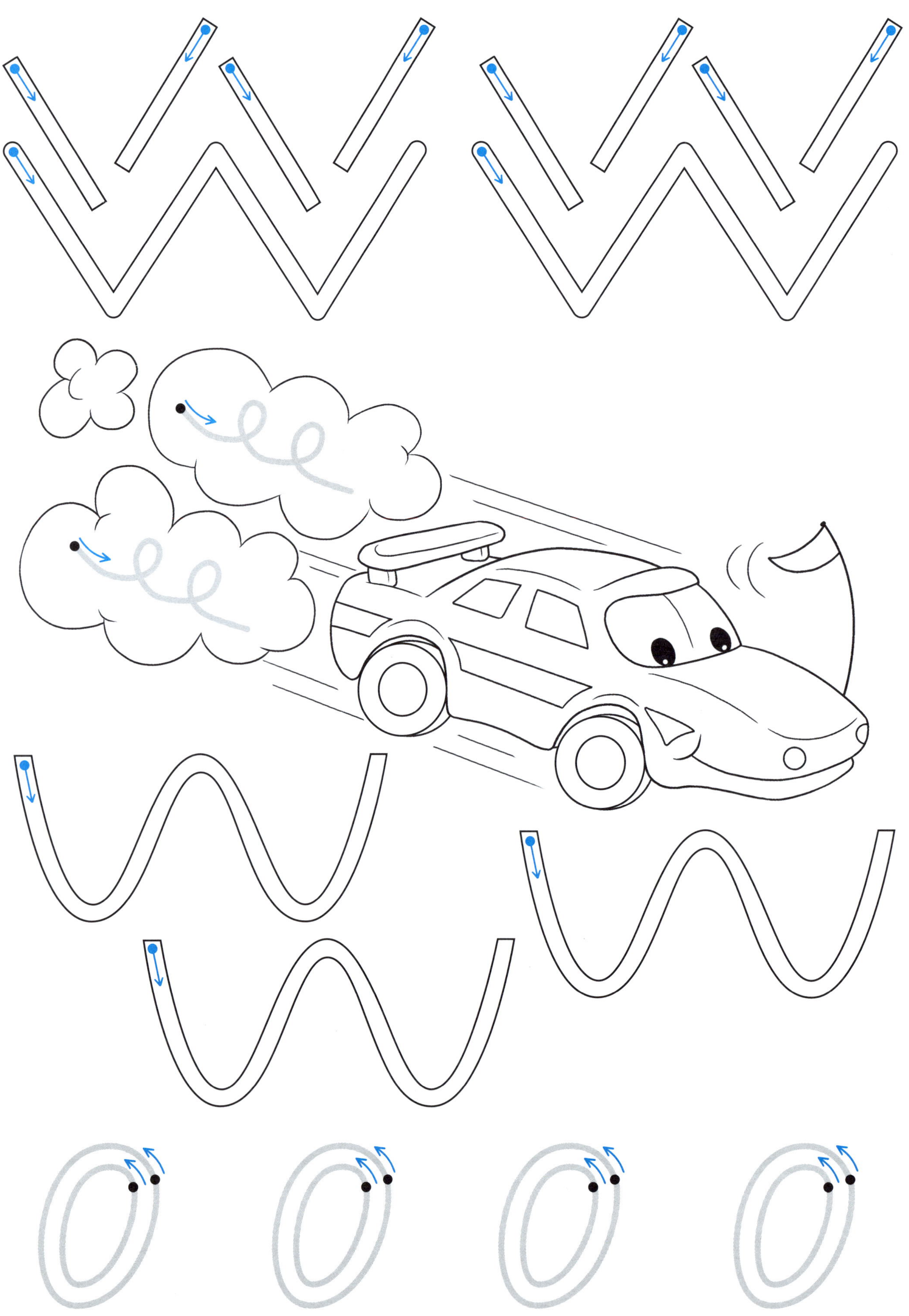

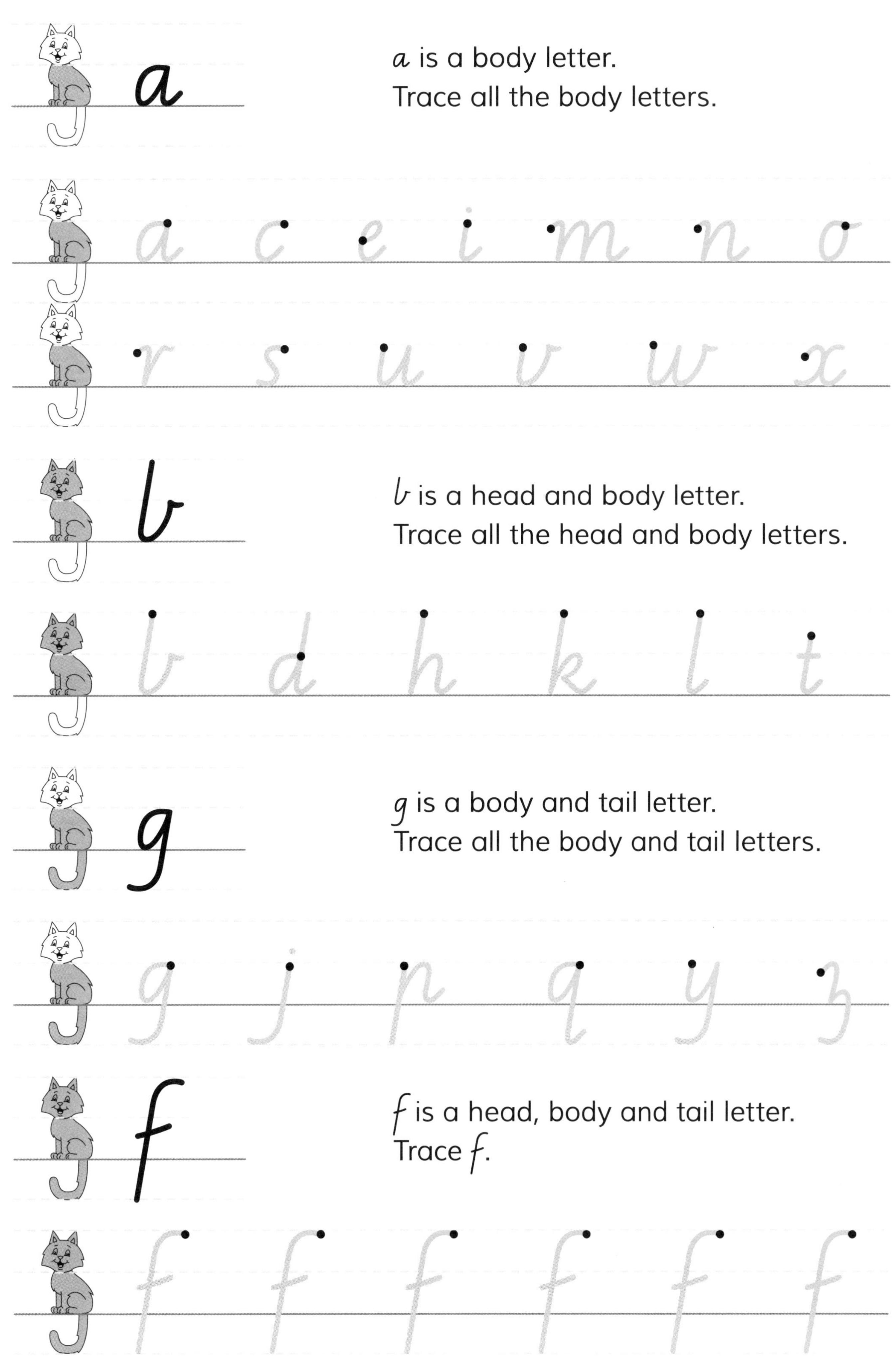

a is a body letter.
Trace all the body letters.

b is a head and body letter.
Trace all the head and body letters.

g is a body and tail letter.
Trace all the body and tail letters.

f is a head, body and tail letter.
Trace f.

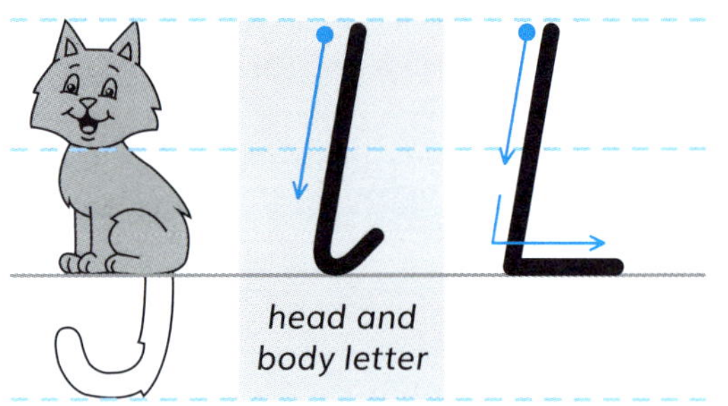

legs

Start at the blue dot. Follow the arrow.

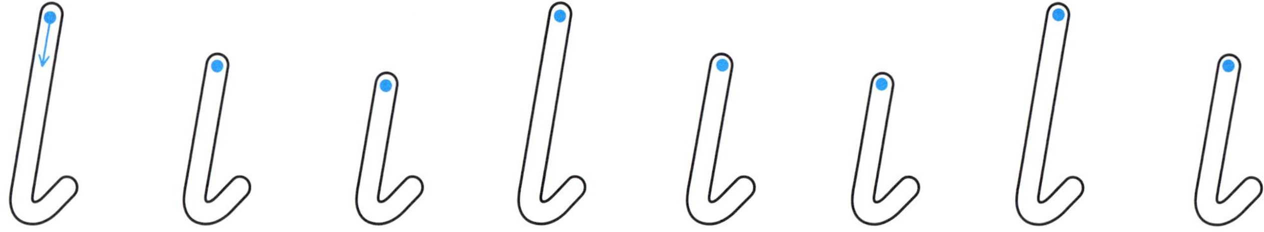

Track the letter.

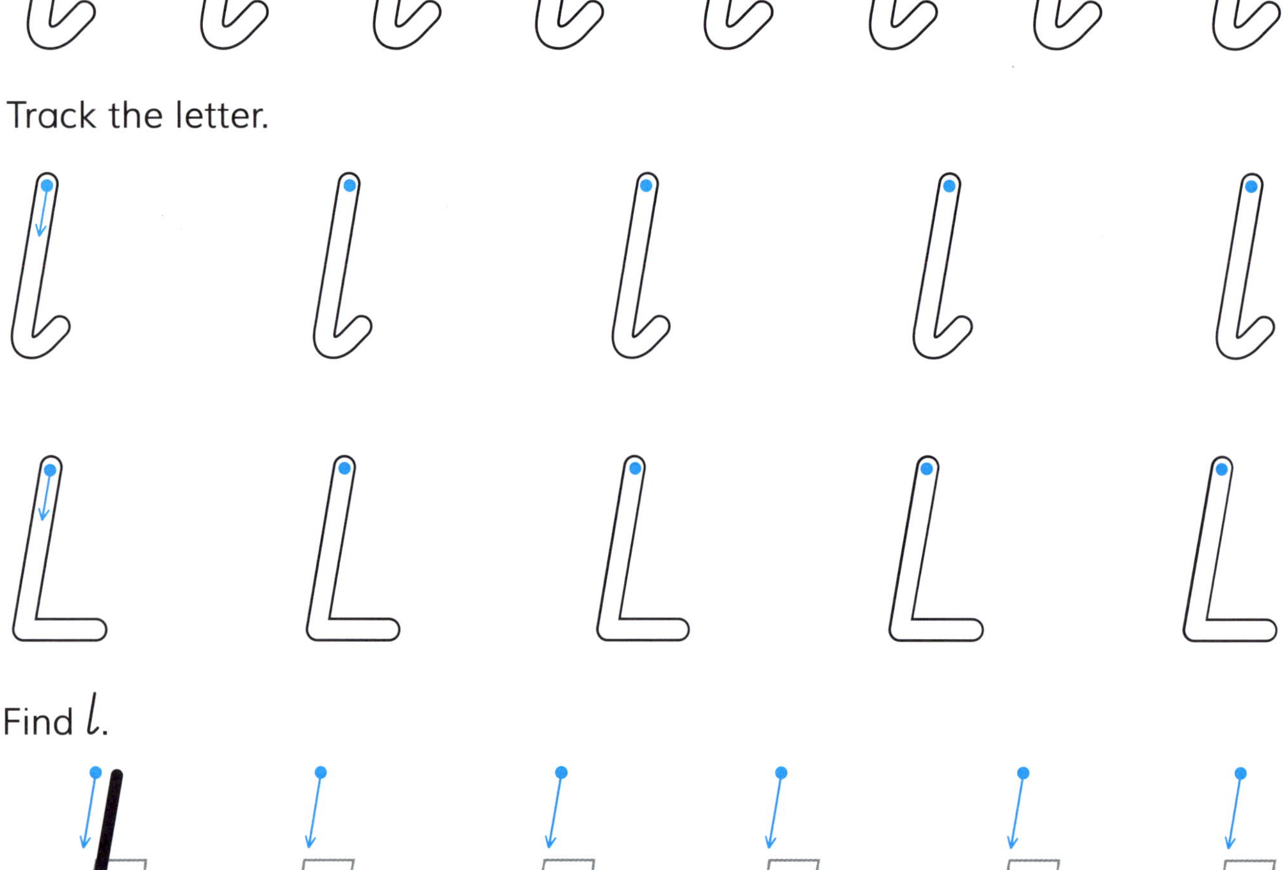

Find l.

Trace and copy. Complete the lines.

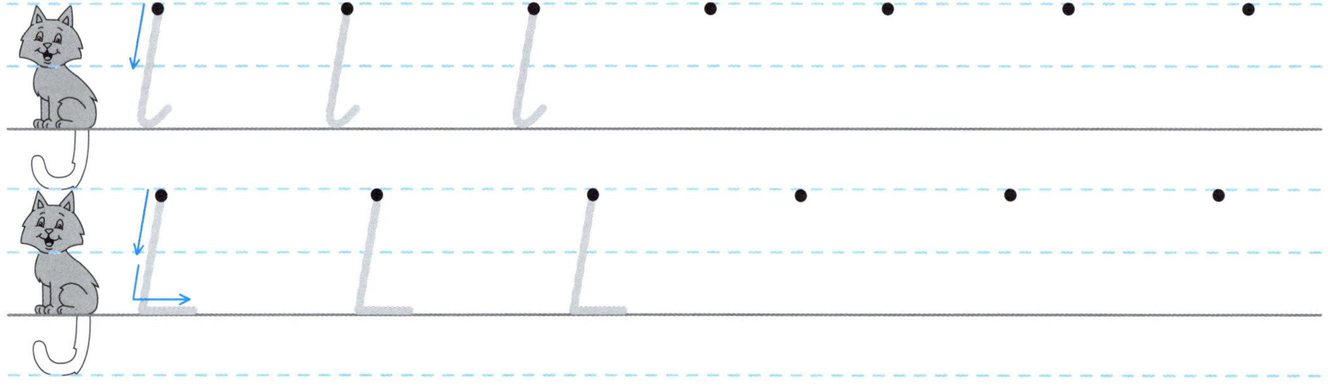

Trace and copy.

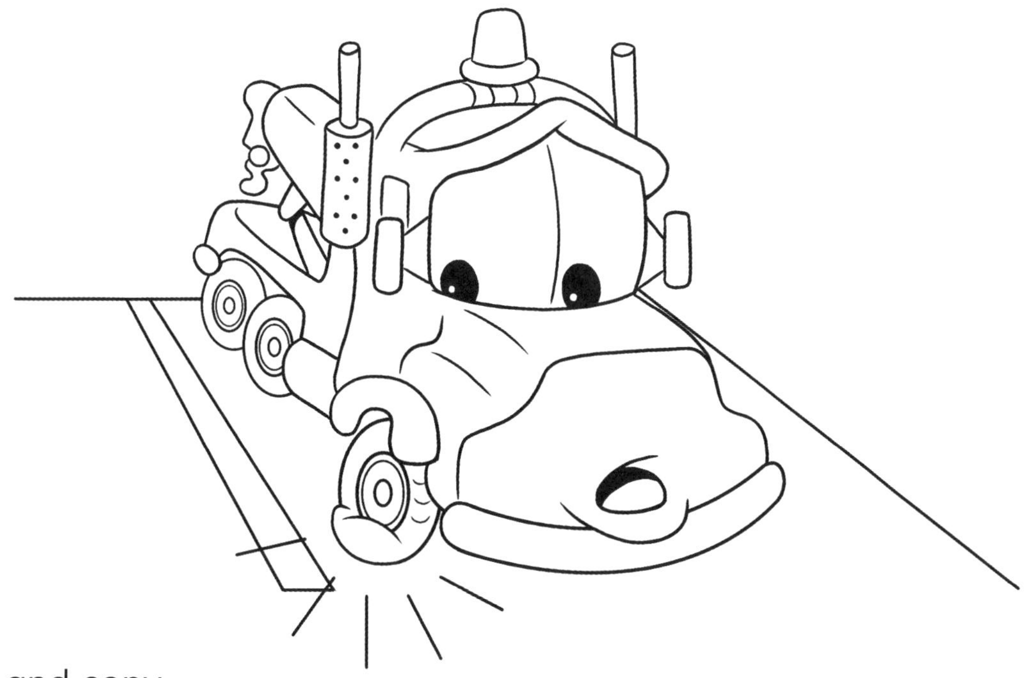

Trace and copy.

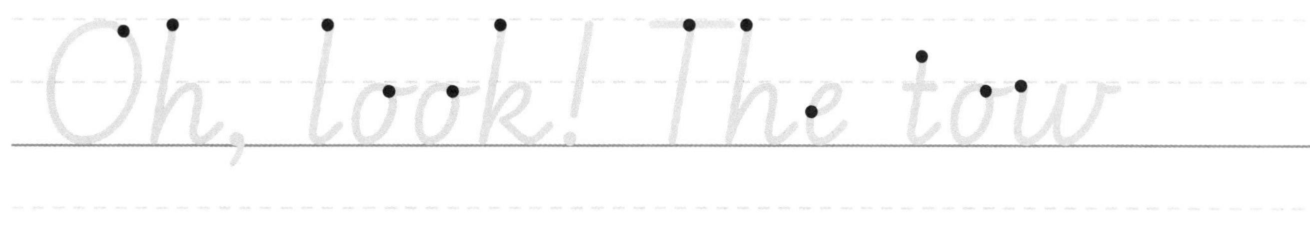

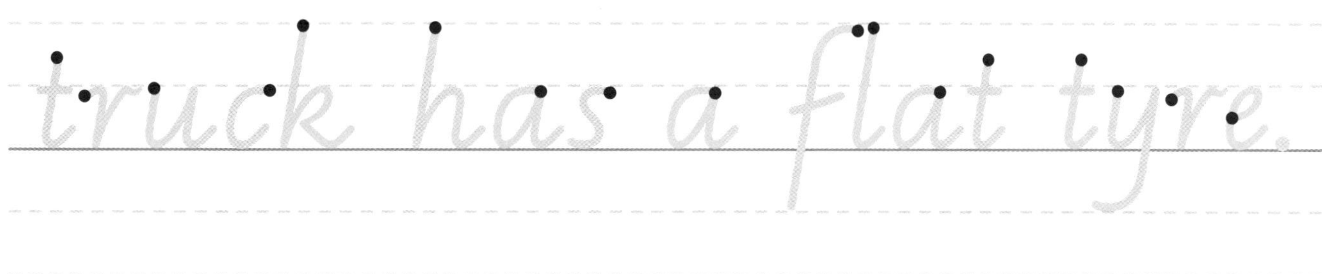

ice cream

Start at the blue dot. Follow the arrow.

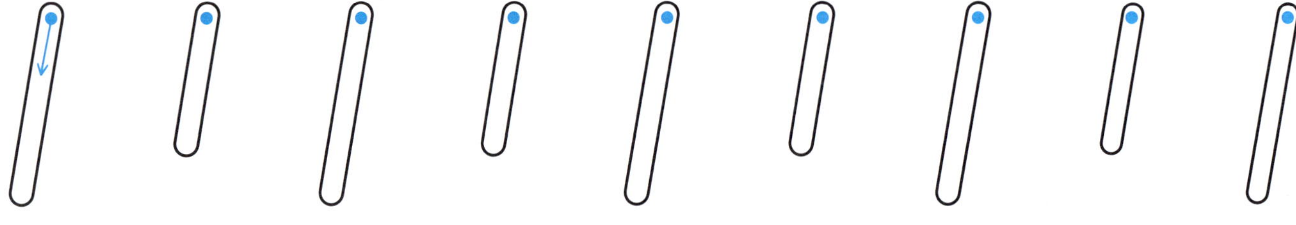

Track the letter.

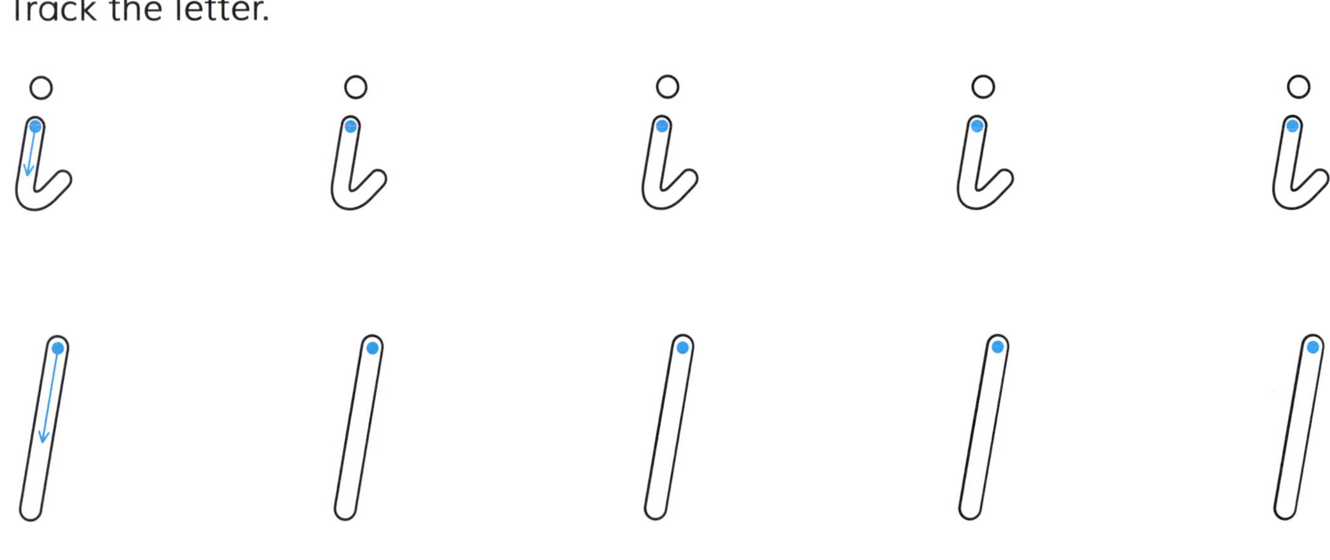

Find *i*.

Trace and copy. Complete the lines.

Trace and copy.

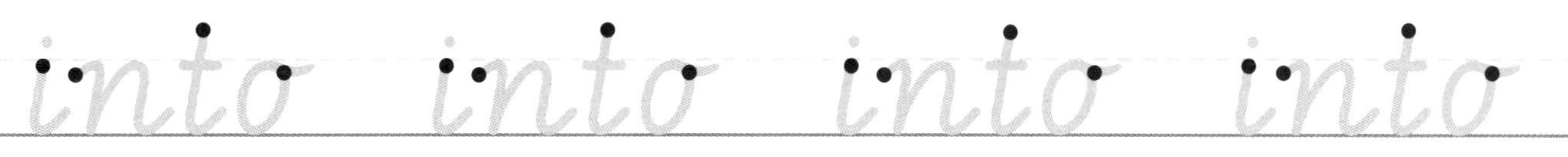

Trace and copy.

"I will put air into

your tyre," said the bus.

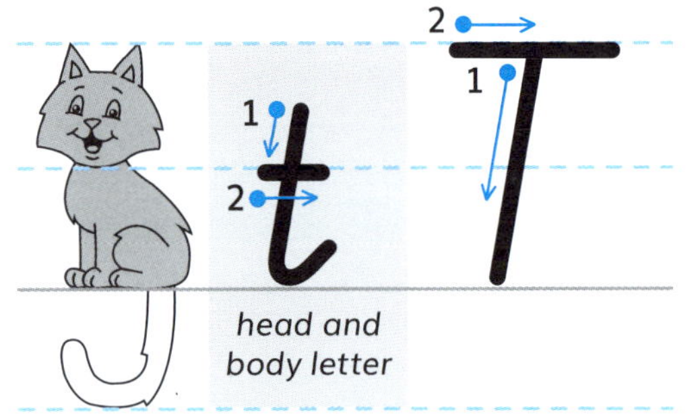

Start at the blue dot. Follow the arrow.

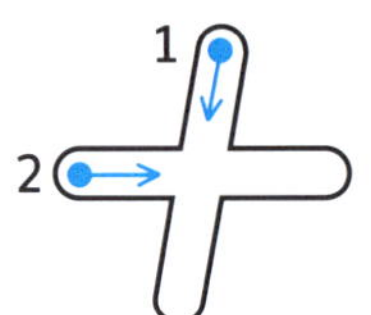

Track the letter.

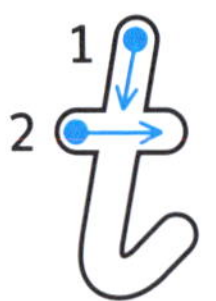

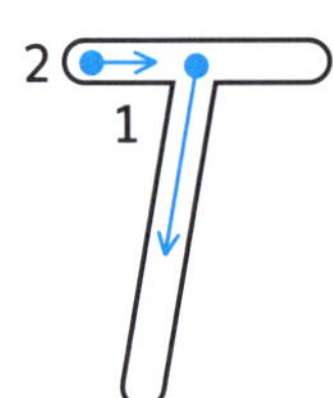
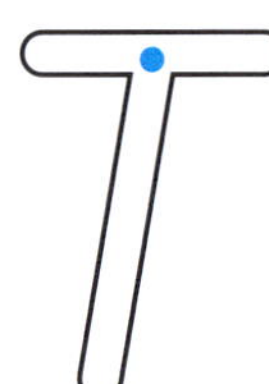
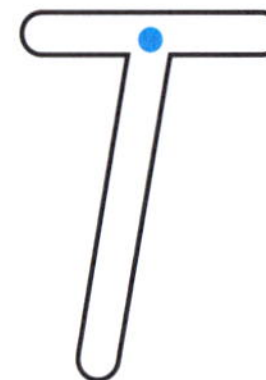

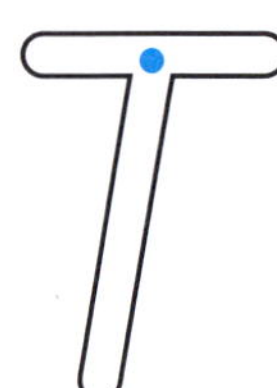

Find *t*.

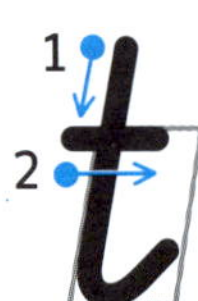
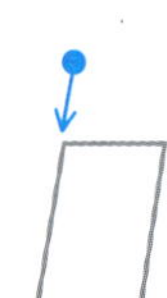
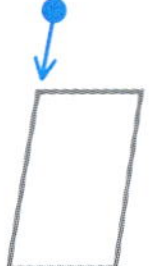
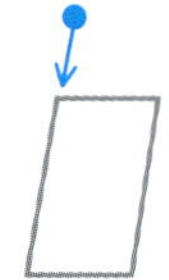
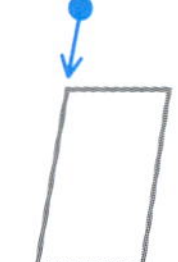

Trace and copy. Complete the lines.

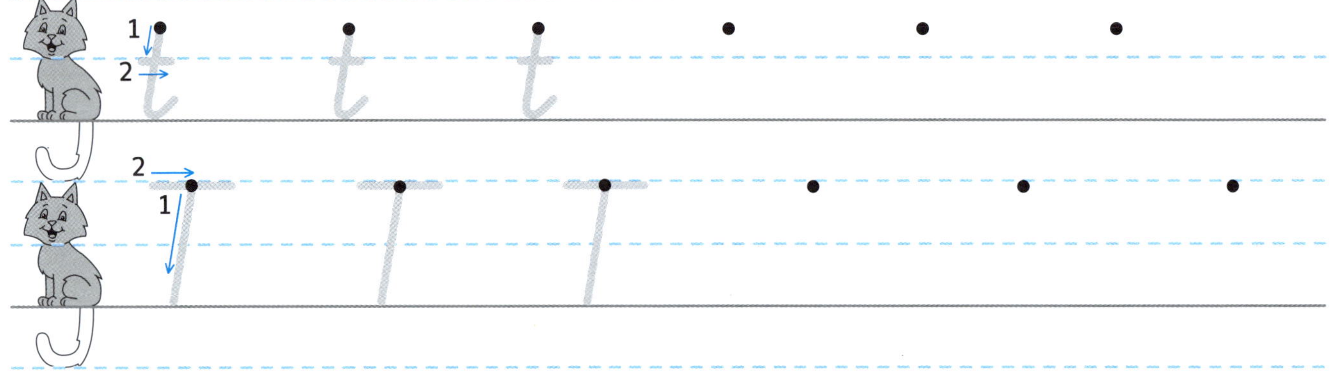

Trace and copy.

thank thank thank

Trace and copy.

"Oh, thank you!"

said the tow truck.

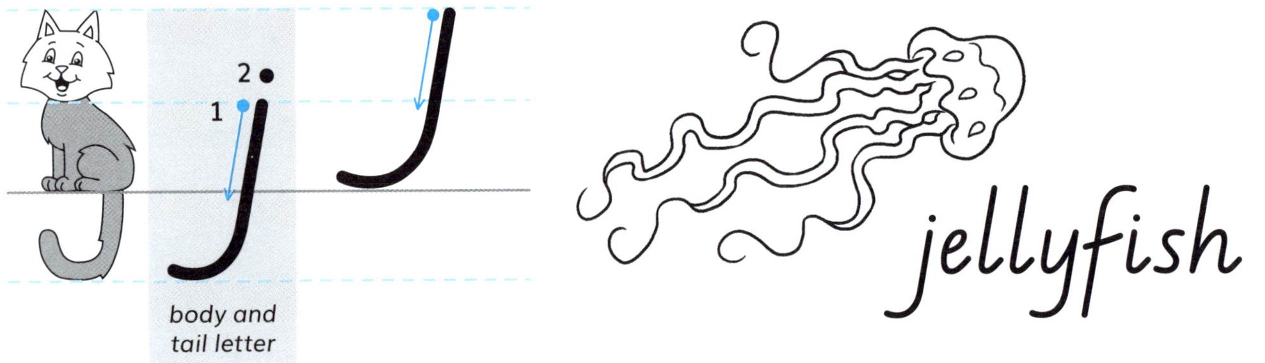

Start at the blue dot. Follow the arrow.

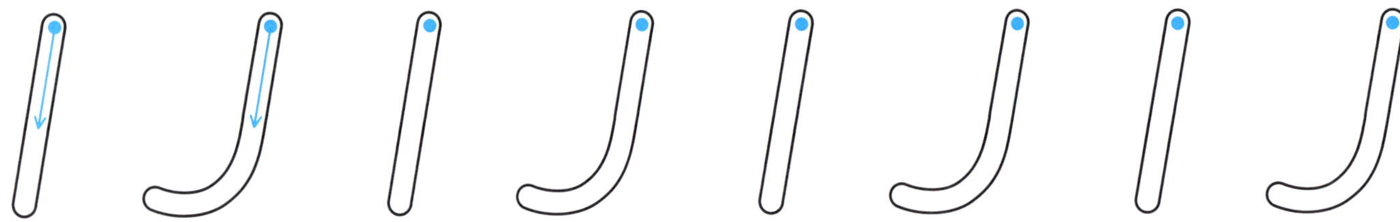

Track the letter.

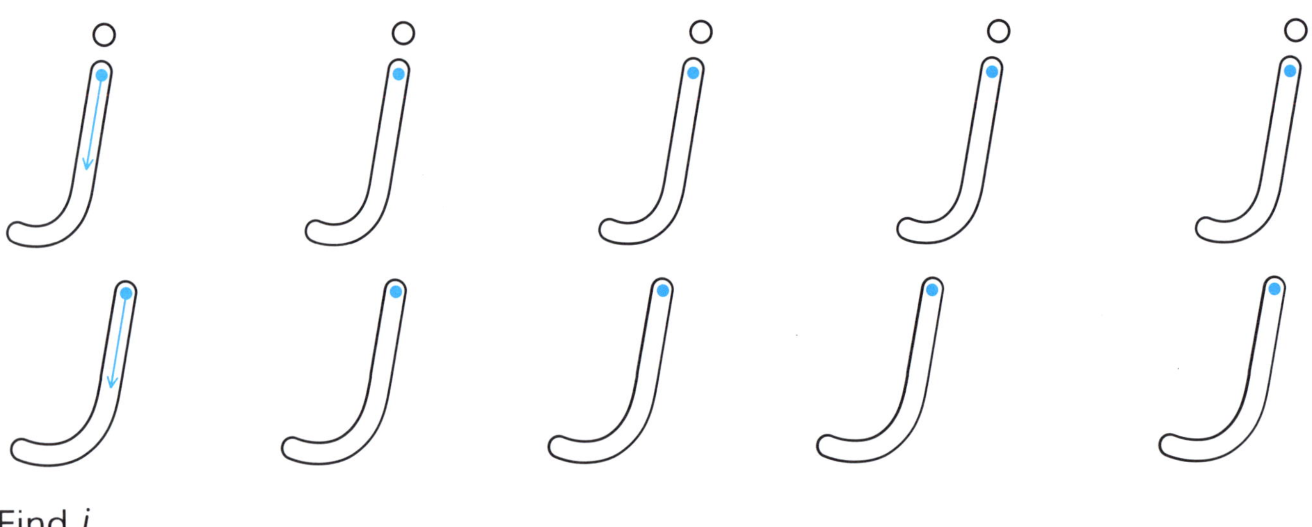

Find *j*.

Trace and copy. Complete the lines.

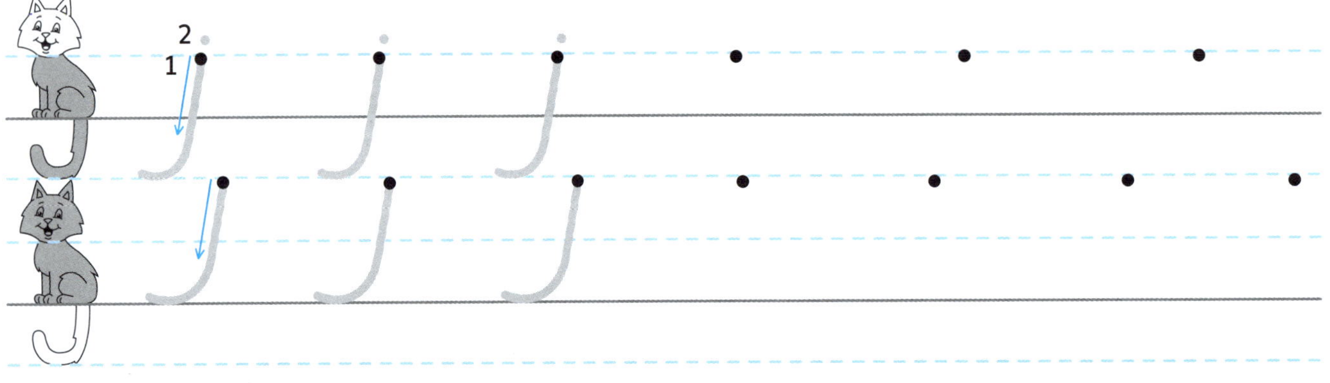

Trace and copy.

job job job job

get.ga/PMWA140

Trace and copy.

"Now I can go

to my next job."

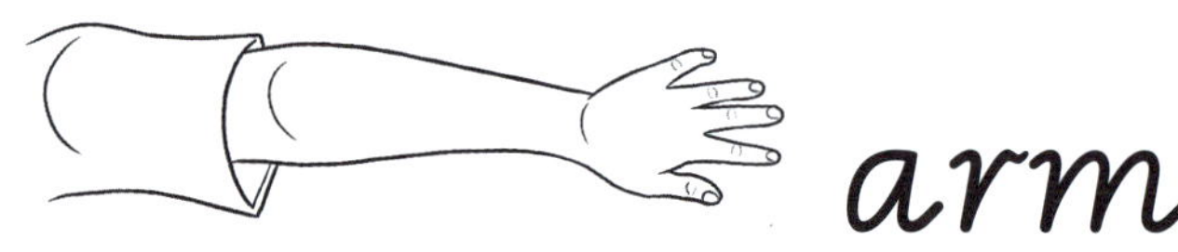

Start at the blue dot. Follow the arrow.

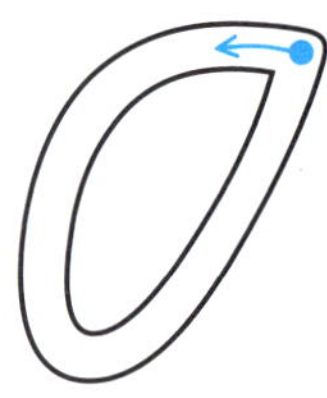  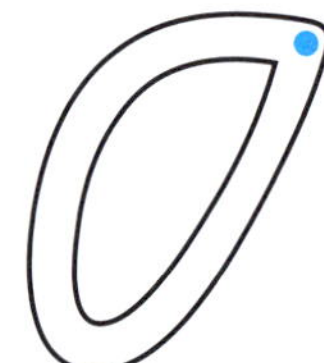 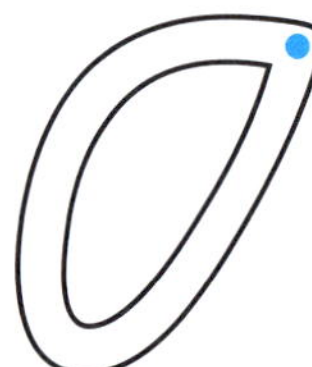 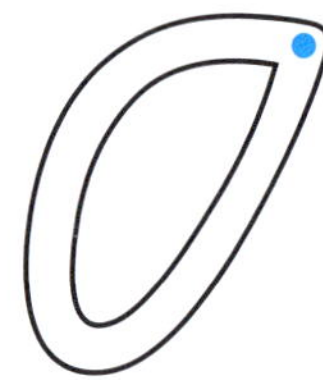

Track the letter.

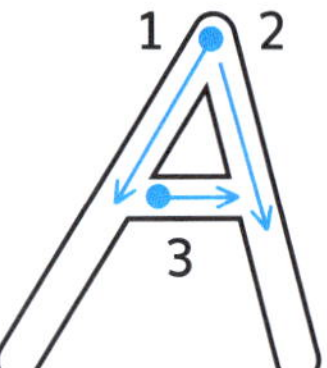

 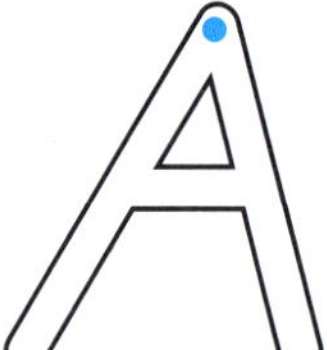  

Find *a* and colour the wedge.

 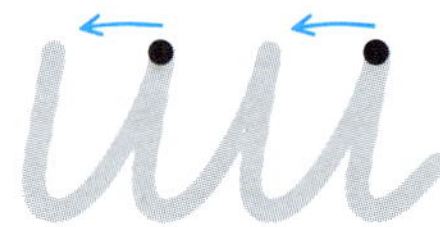  

Trace and copy. Complete the lines.

Trace and copy.

around around

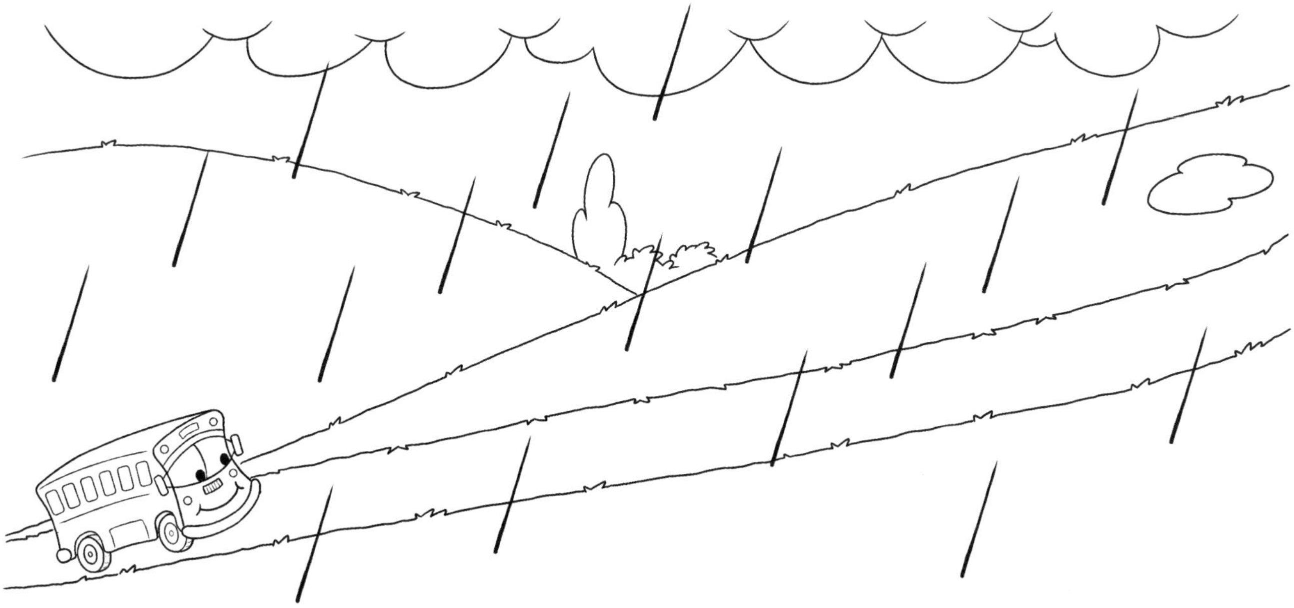

Trace and copy.

The bus was driving

around Toytown.

duck

Start at the blue dot. Follow the arrow.

Track the letter.

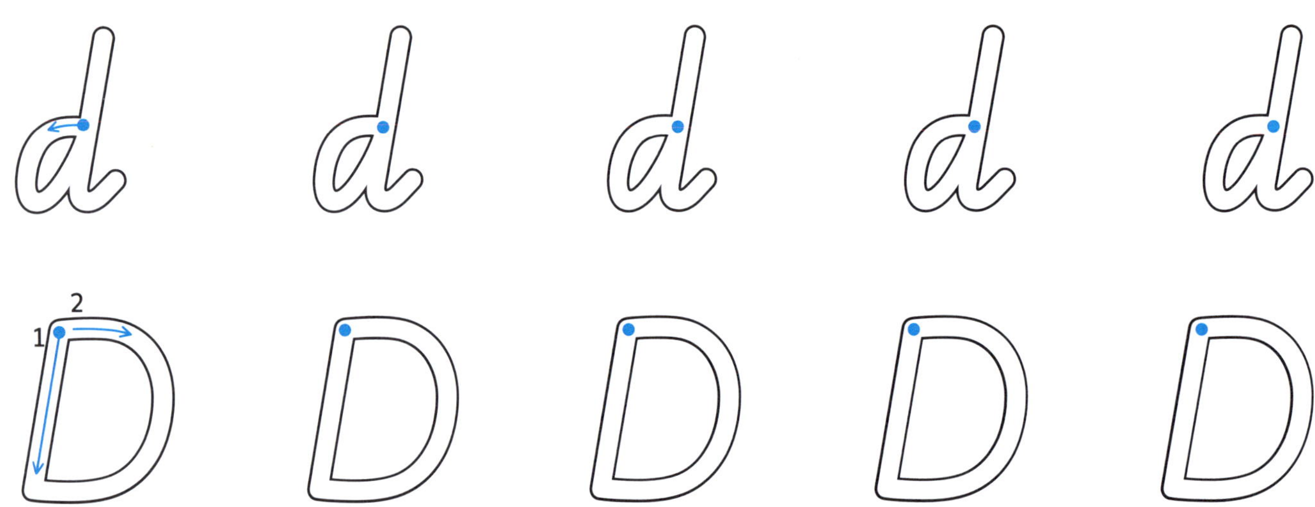

Find *d* and colour the wedge.

Trace and copy. Complete the lines.

Trace and copy.

down down down

Trace and copy.

The racing car

skidded down the hill.

Start at the blue dot. Follow the arrow.

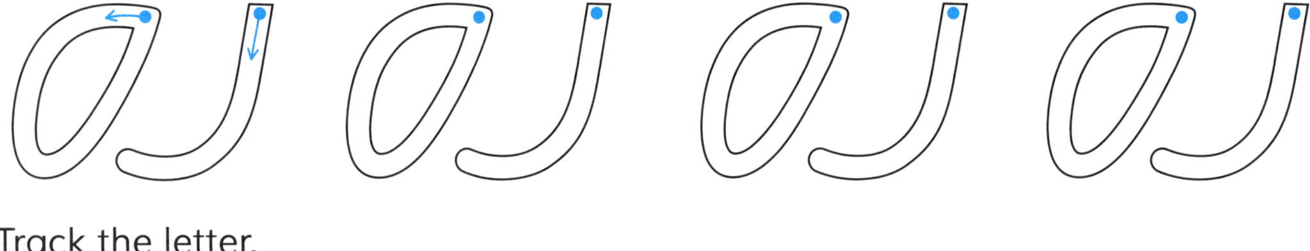

Track the letter.

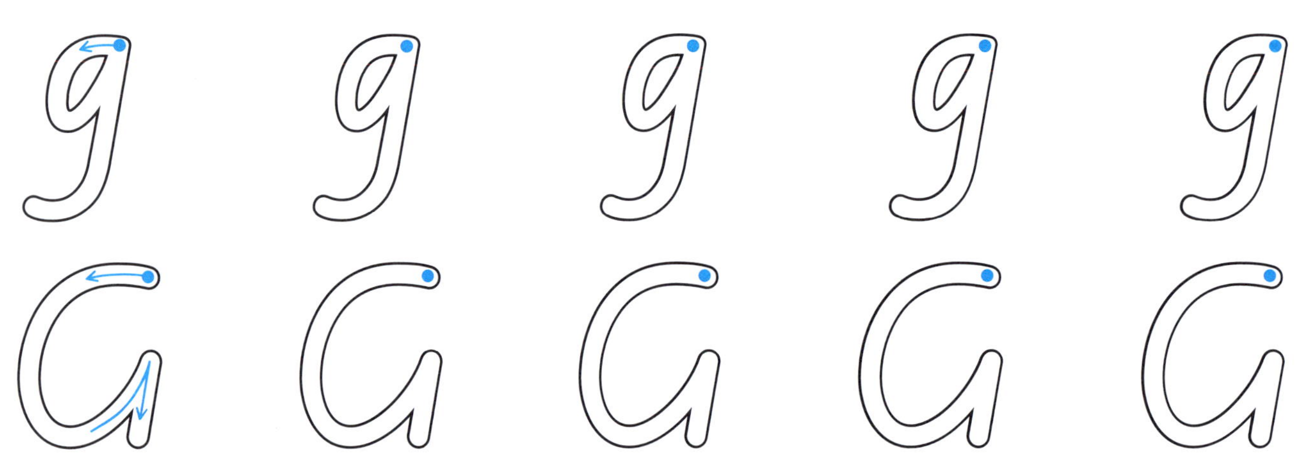

Find *g* and colour the wedge.

Trace and copy. Complete the lines.

Trace and copy.

get get get get

Trace and copy.

Crash! "I must get

help!" said the bus.

Start at the blue dot. Follow the arrow.

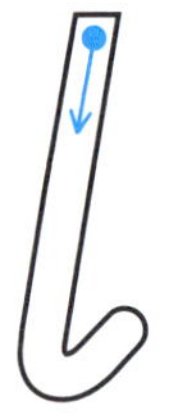    

Track the letter.

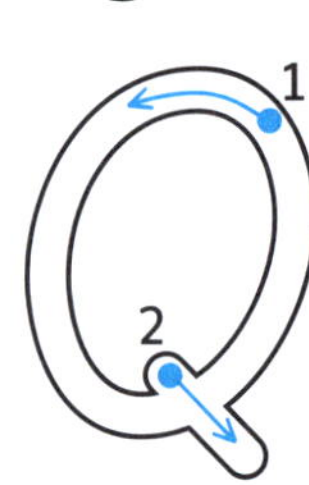 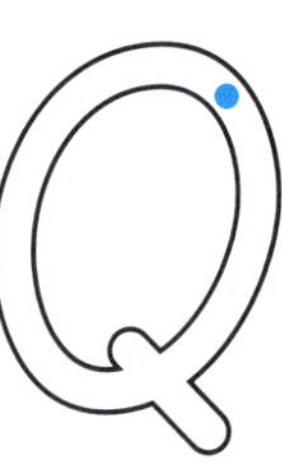 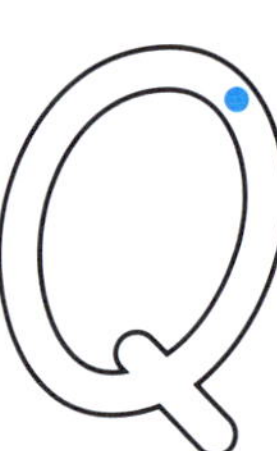  

Find *q* and colour the wedge.

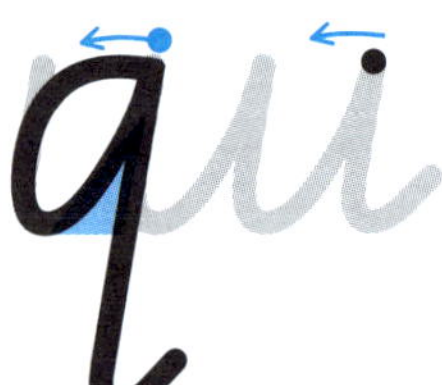  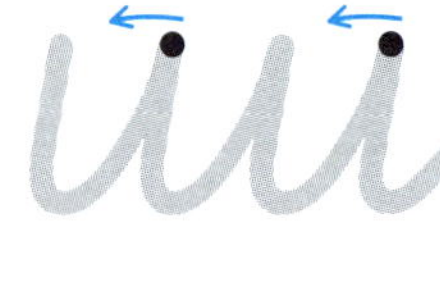 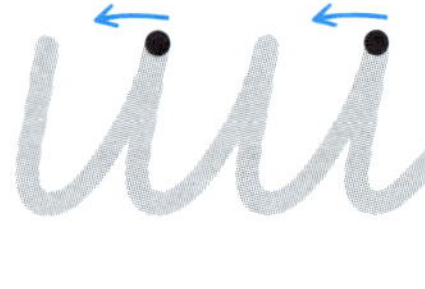

Trace and copy. Complete the lines.

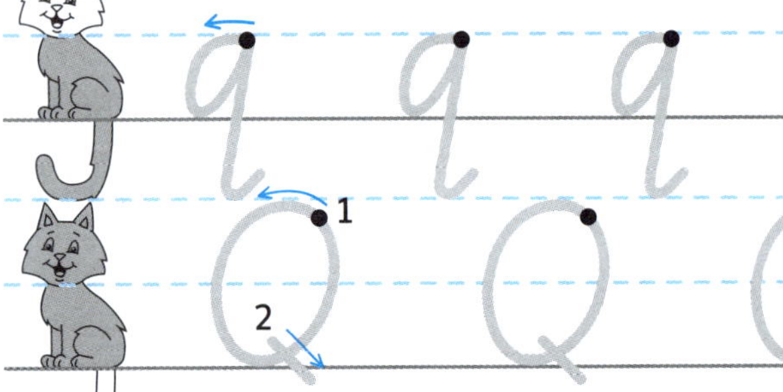

Trace and copy.

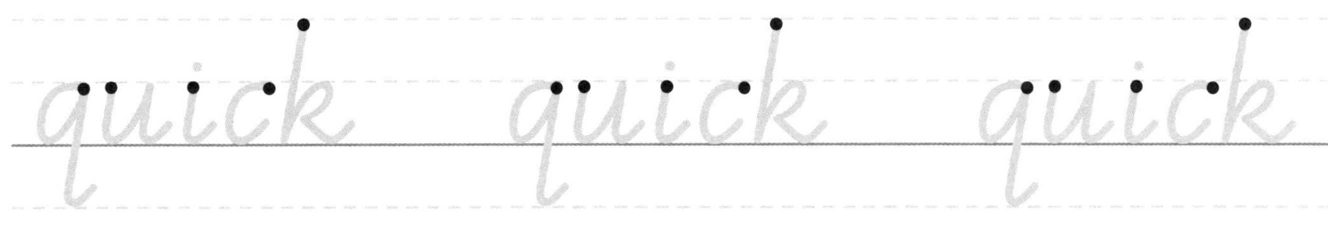

Trace and copy.

truck. "Be quick!"

ISBN: 9780170424035

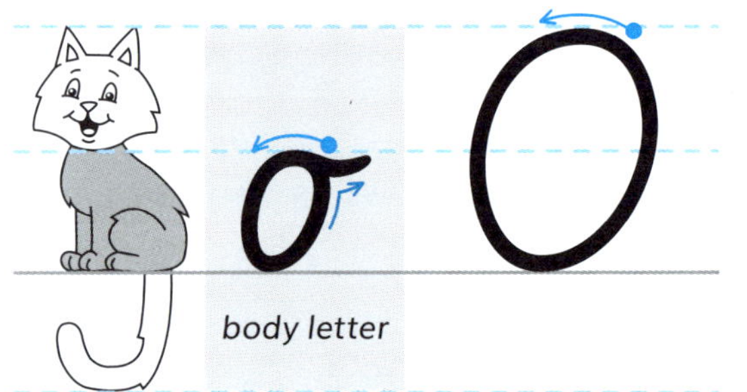

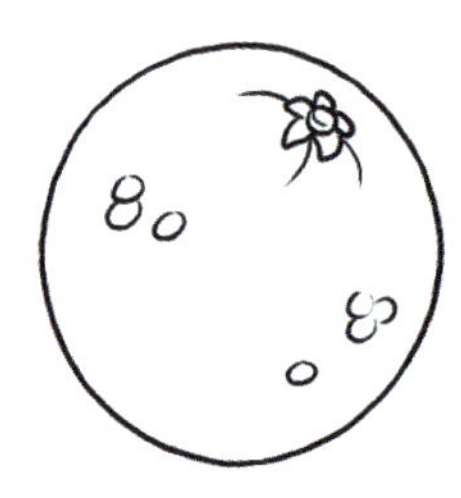

orange

Start at the blue dot. Follow the arrow.

Track the letter.

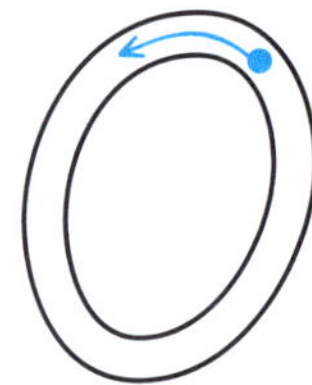 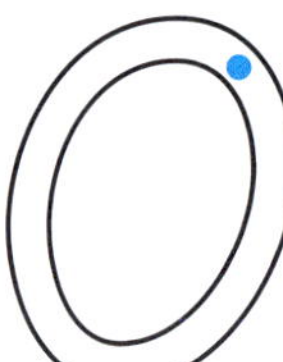 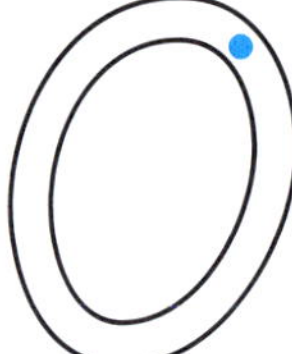 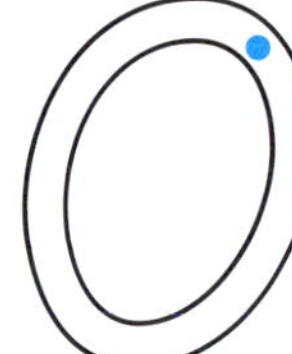 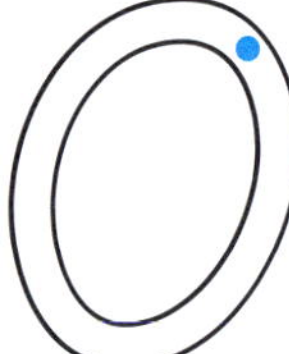

Find *o*.

 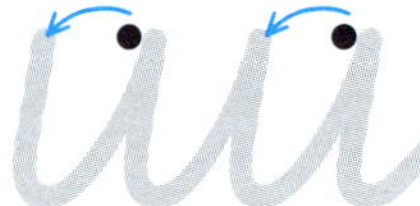  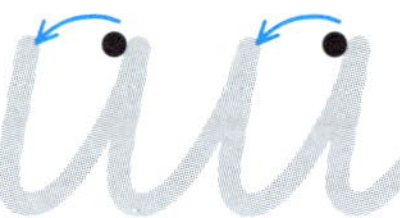

Trace and copy. Complete the lines.

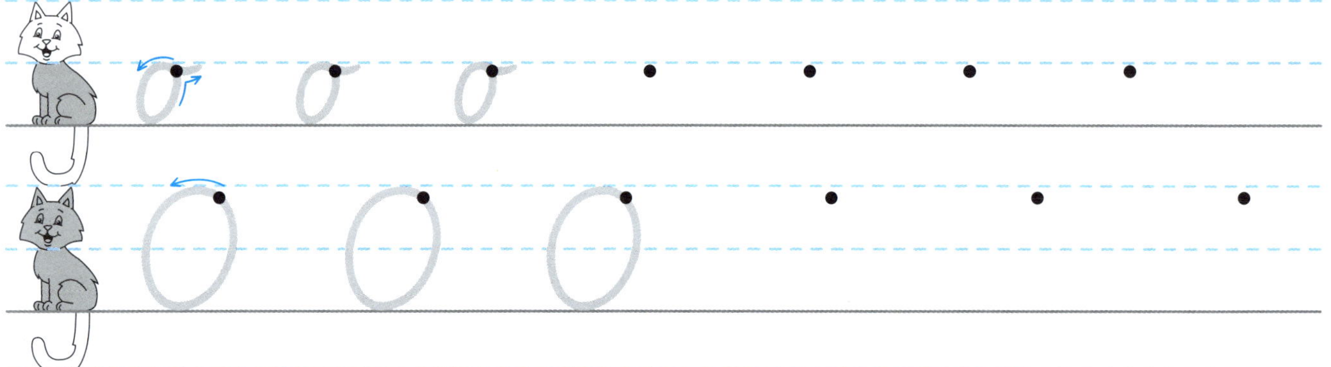

Trace and copy.

out out out out

Trace and copy.

How will the racing

car get out?

get.ga/PMWA141

ISBN: 9780170424035

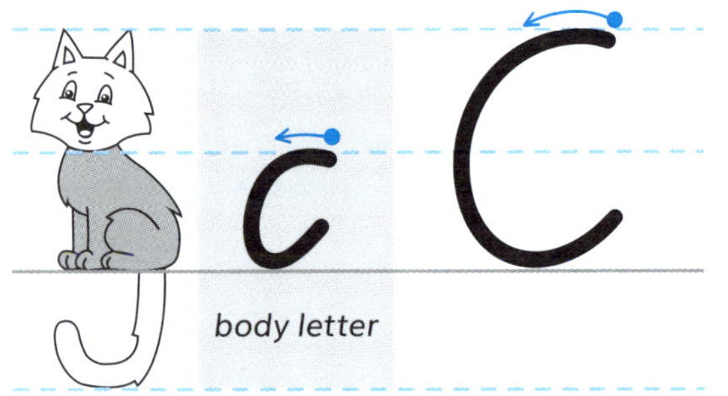

carrot

Start at the blue dot. Follow the arrow.

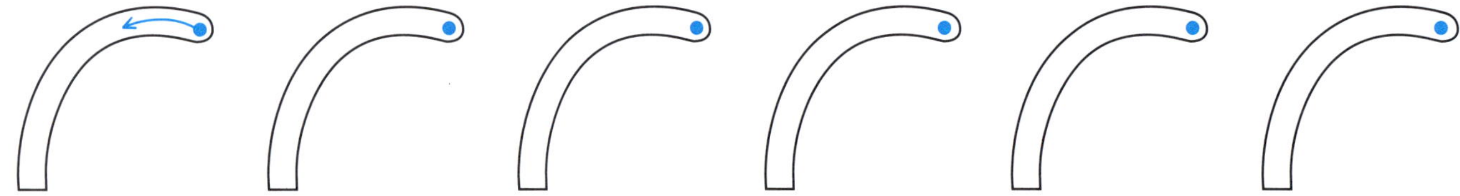

Track the letter.

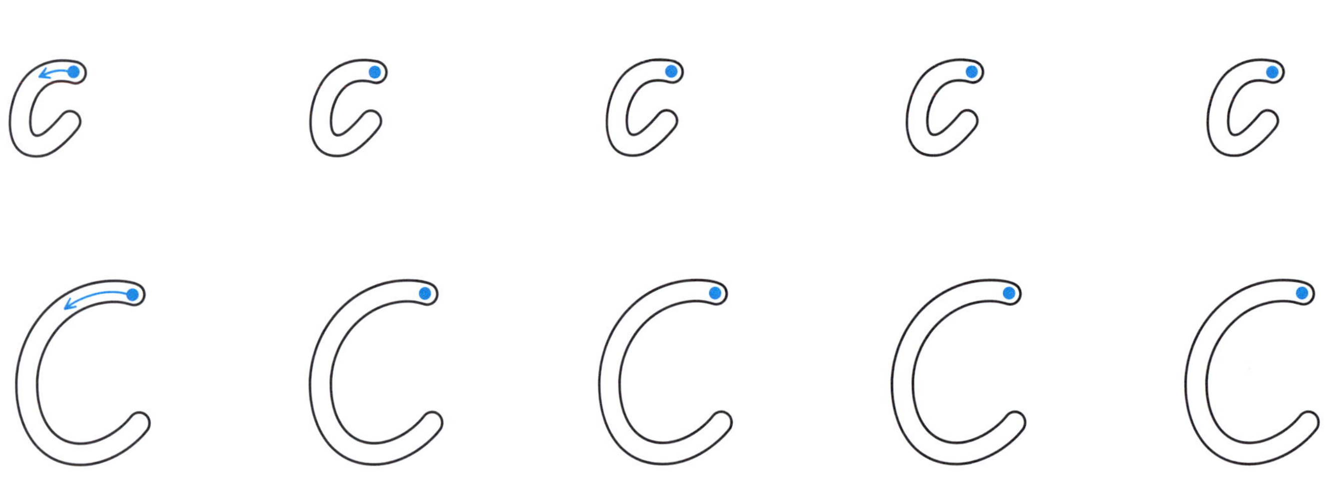

Find *c*.

Trace and copy. Complete the lines.

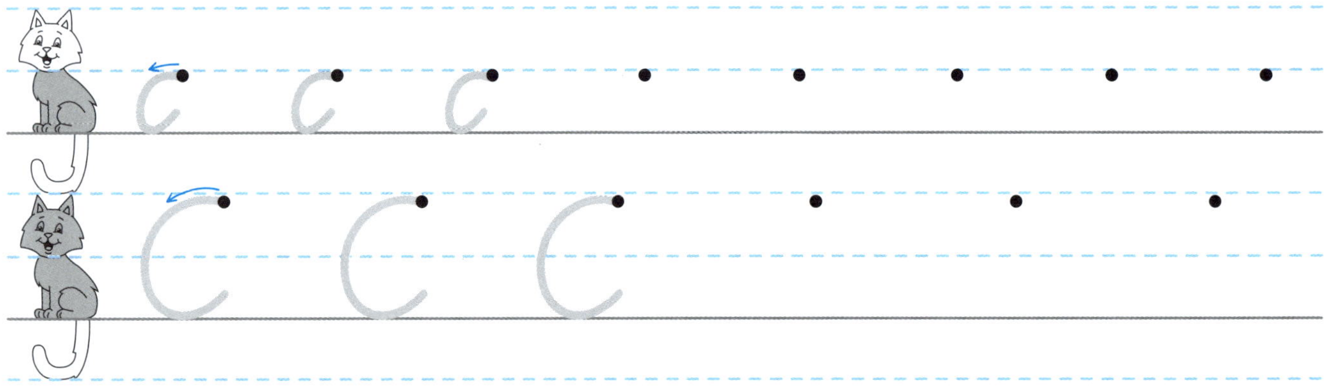

Trace and copy.

came came came

Trace and copy.

The tow truck came

to the rescue.

ISBN: 9780170424035

Start at the blue dot. Follow the arrow.

Track the letter.

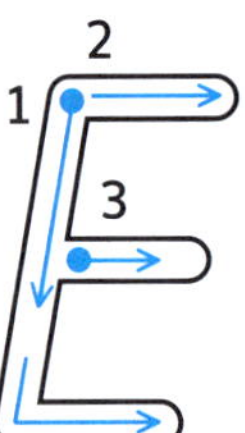

Find *e*.

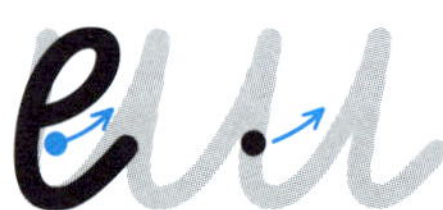

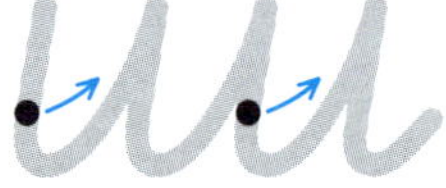

Trace and copy. Complete the lines.

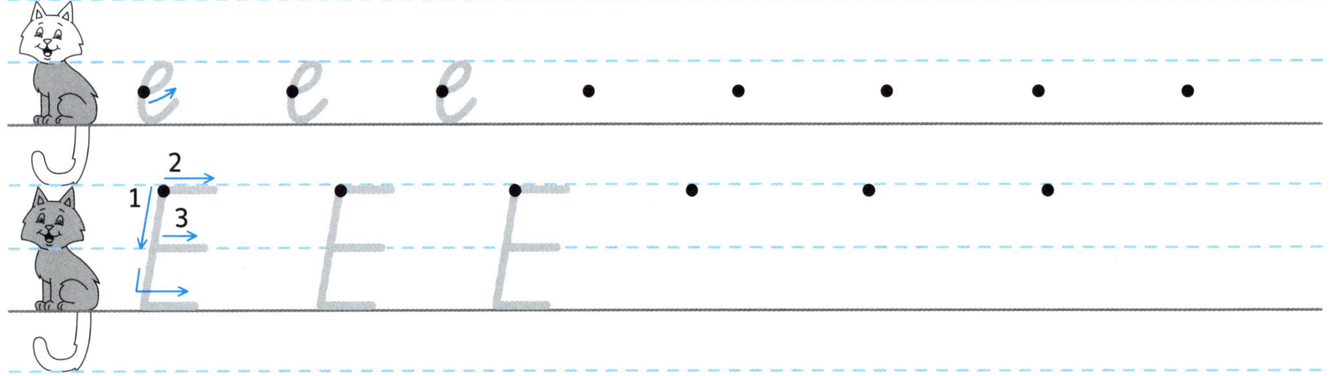

ISBN: 9780170424035

Trace and copy.

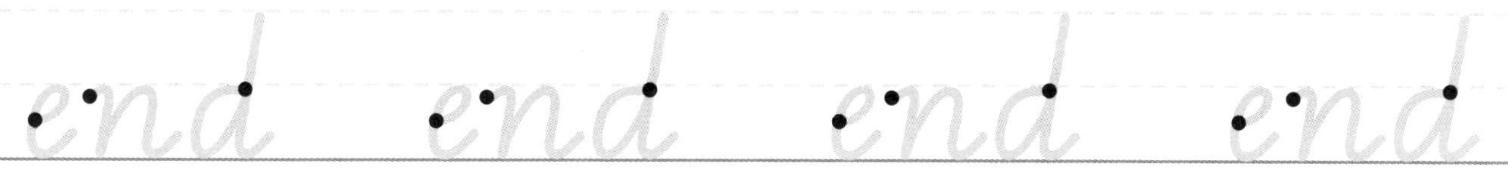

Trace and copy.

of my rope," he said.

shoe

Start at the blue dot. Follow the arrow.

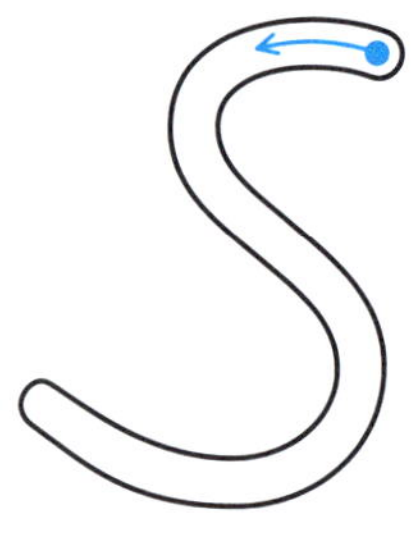 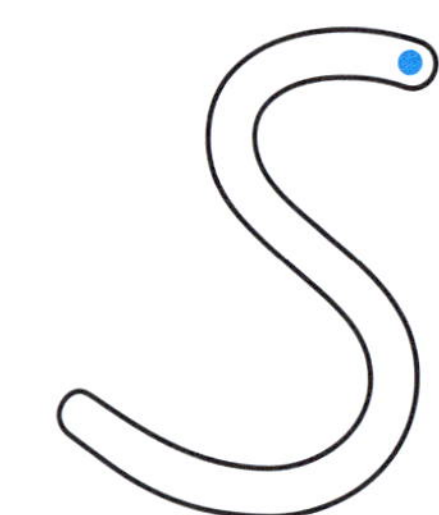  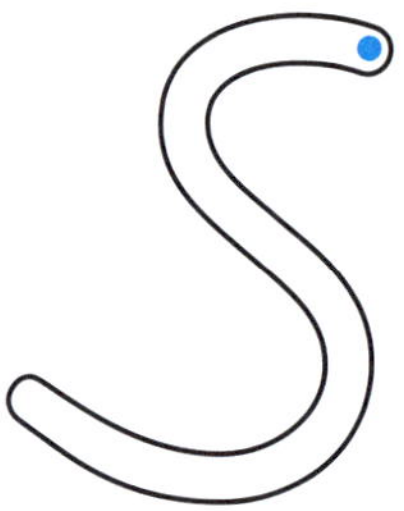

Track the letter.

 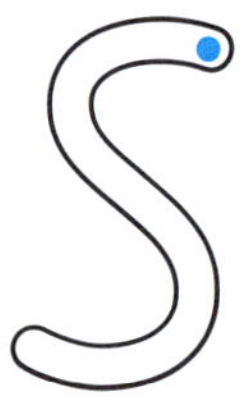   

Find *s*.

 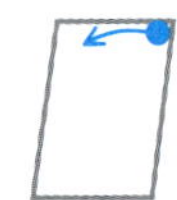    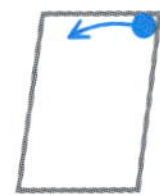

Trace and copy. Complete the lines.

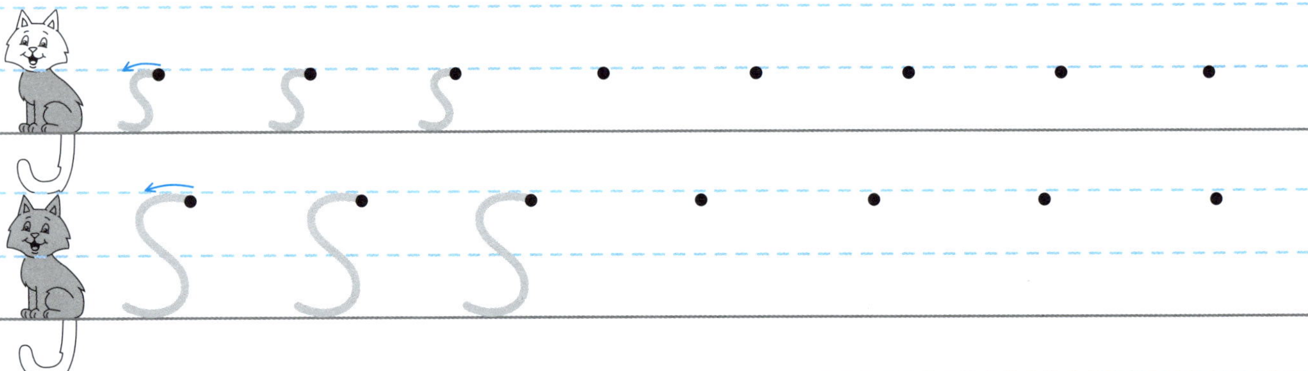
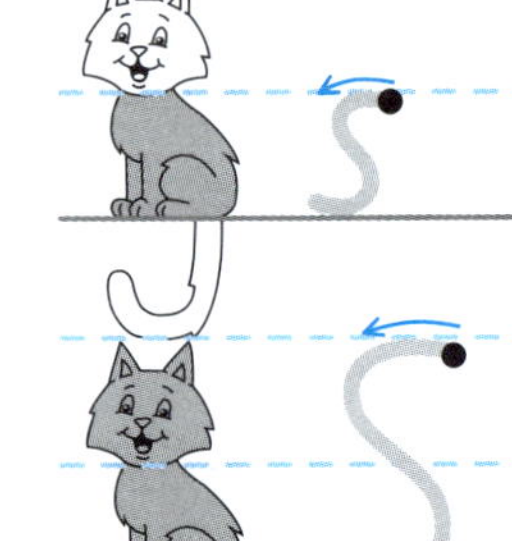
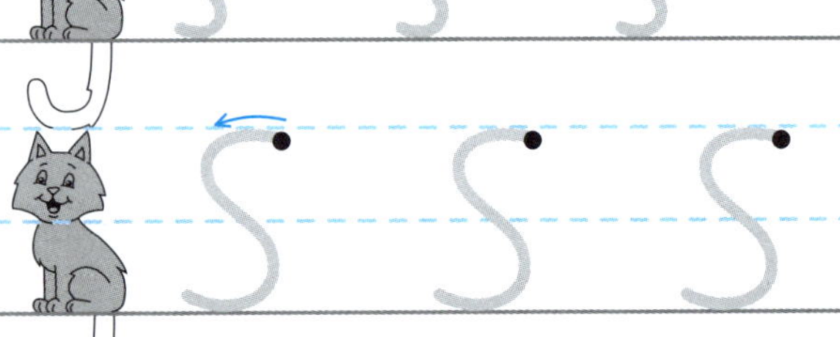

Trace and copy.

said said said said

Trace and copy.

The tow truck pulled.

"Hold tight!" he said.

ISBN: 9780170424035

Start at the blue dot. Follow the arrow.

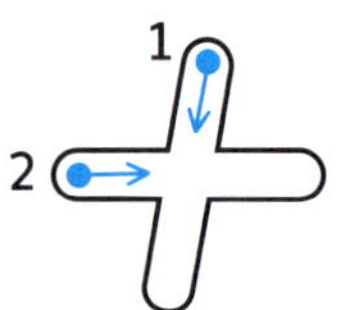    

Track the letter.

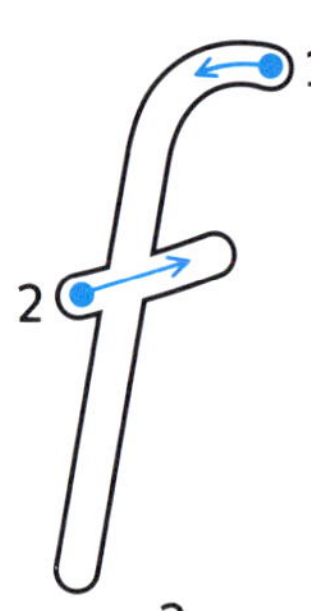   

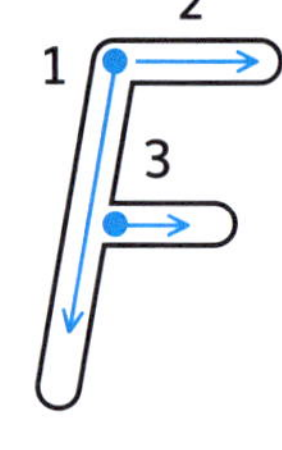    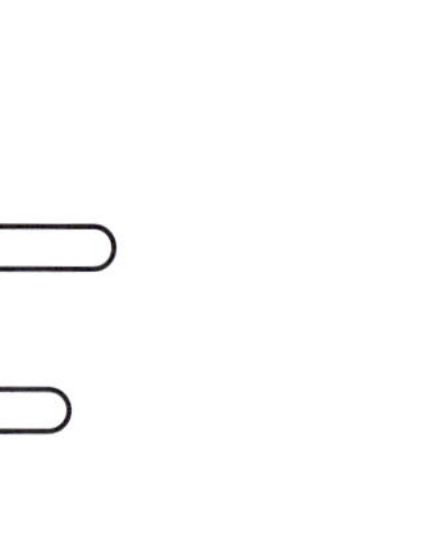 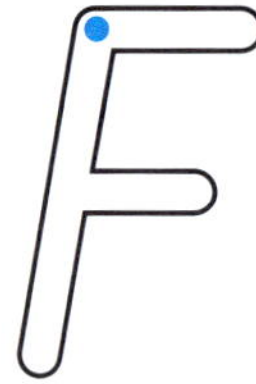 

Find *f*.

Trace and copy. Complete the lines.

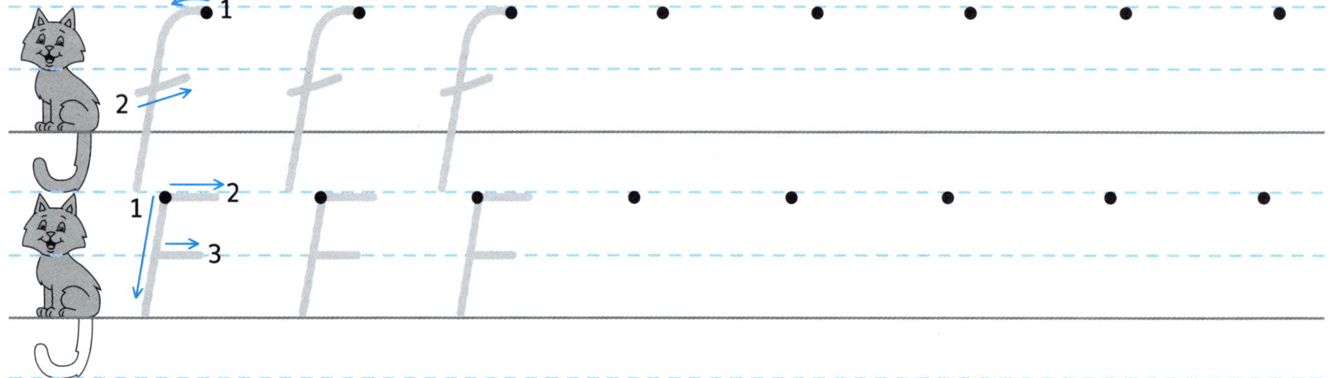

Trace and copy.

for for for for

Trace and copy.

"Thanks for helping!"

said the racing car.

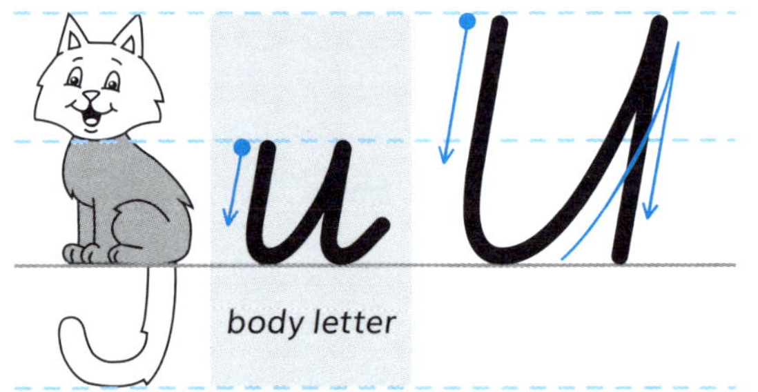

Start at the blue dot. Follow the arrow.

Track the letter.

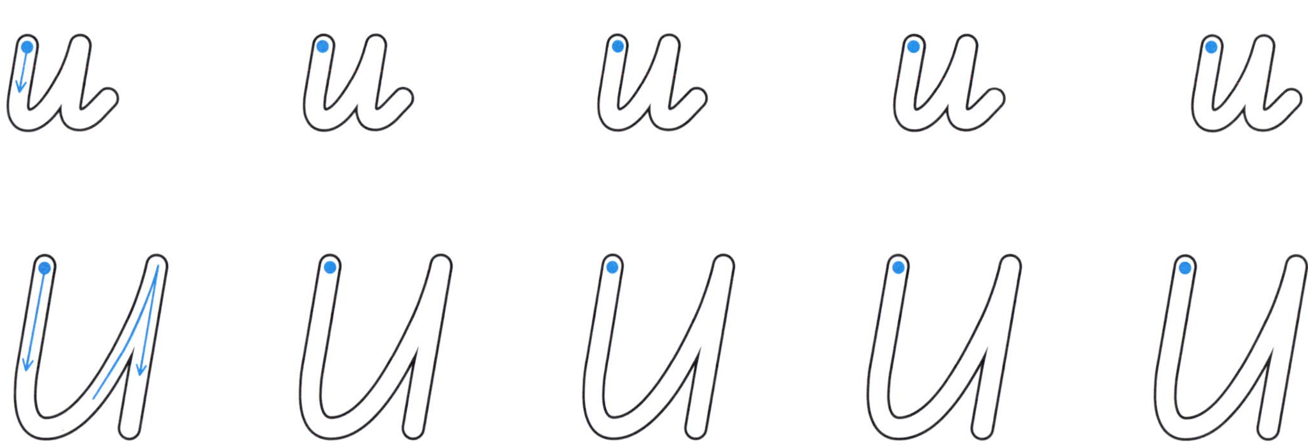

Find *u* and colour the wedge.

Trace and copy. Complete the lines.

Trace and copy.

up up up up

Trace and copy.

get.ga/PMWA142

The racing car drove

away, up the hill.

yawn

Start at the blue dot. Follow the arrow.

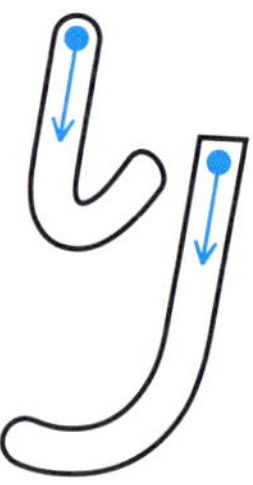

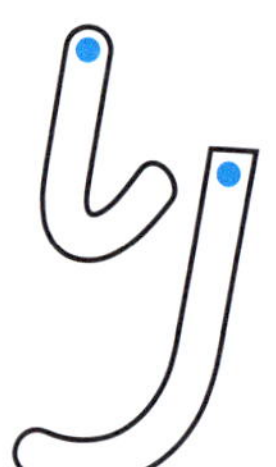

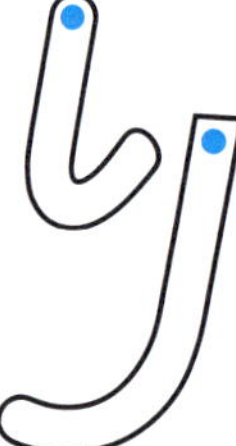

Track the letter.

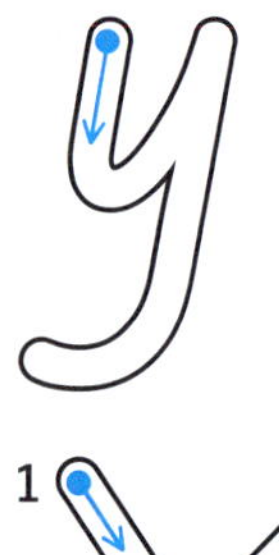
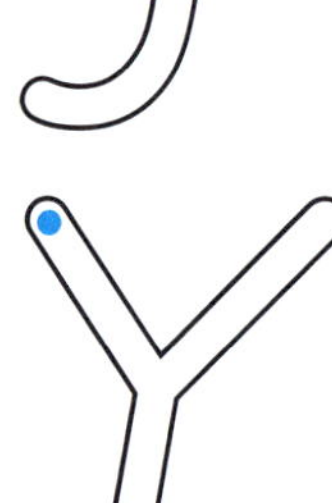
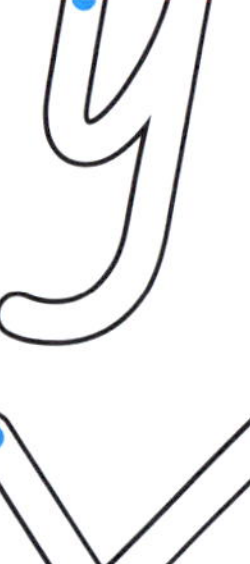

Find *y* and colour the wedge.

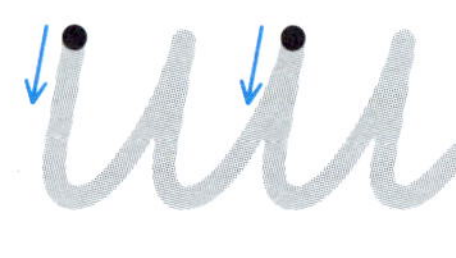

Trace and copy. Complete the lines.

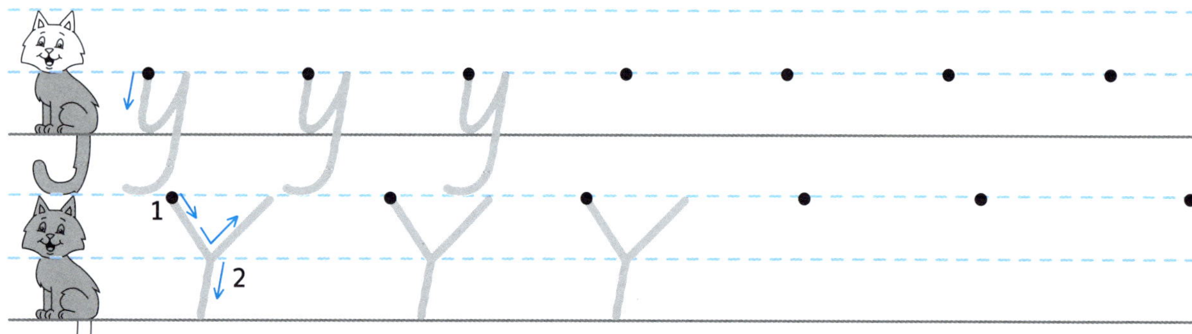

Trace and copy.

yet yet yet yet

Trace and copy.

"Oh, I am not at the

top of the hill yet."

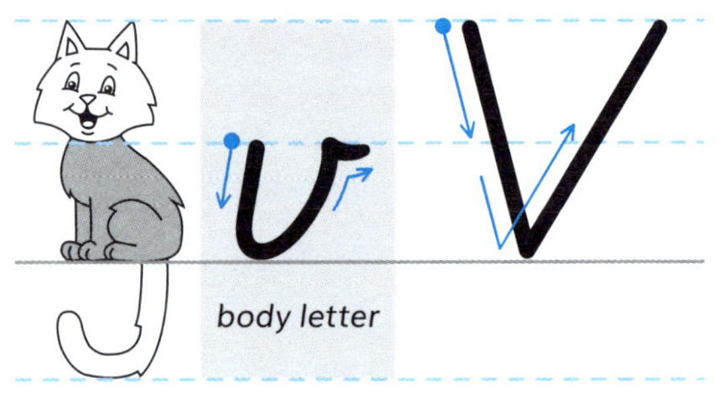

vase

Start at the blue dot. Follow the arrow.

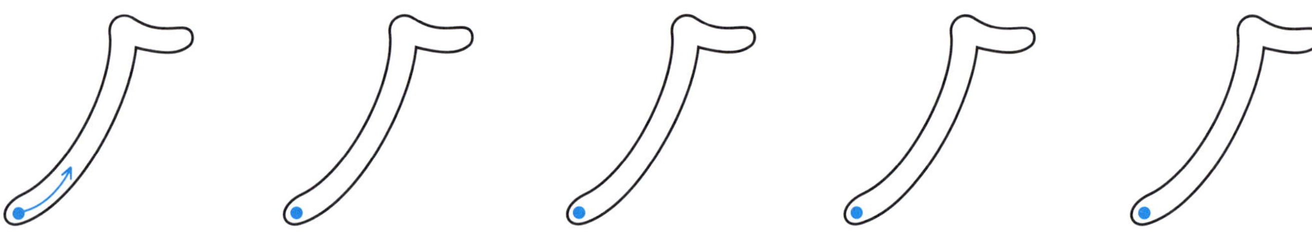

Track the letter.

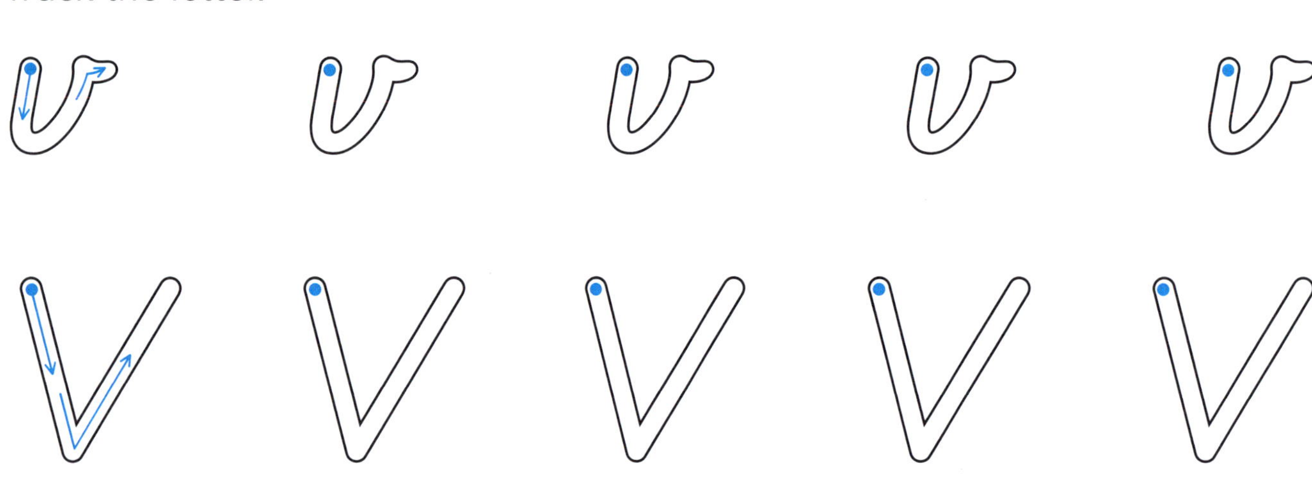

Find *v*.

Trace and copy. Complete the lines.

Trace and copy.

very very very very

Trace and copy.

The bus was very

wet from the rain.

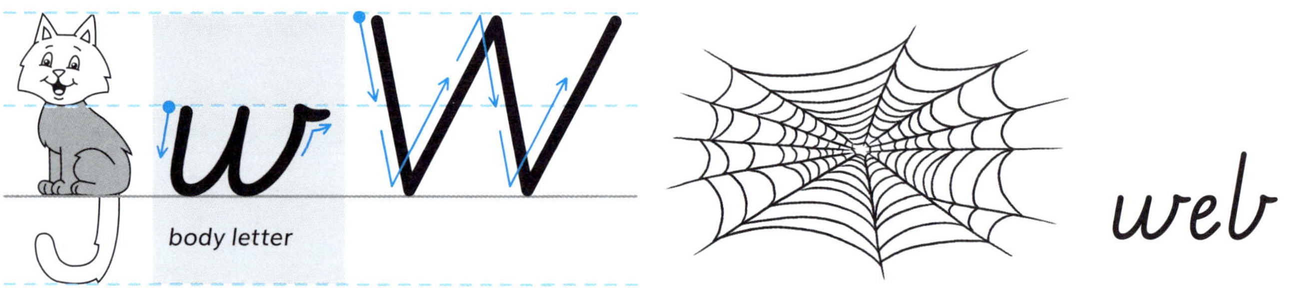

Start at the blue dot. Follow the arrow.

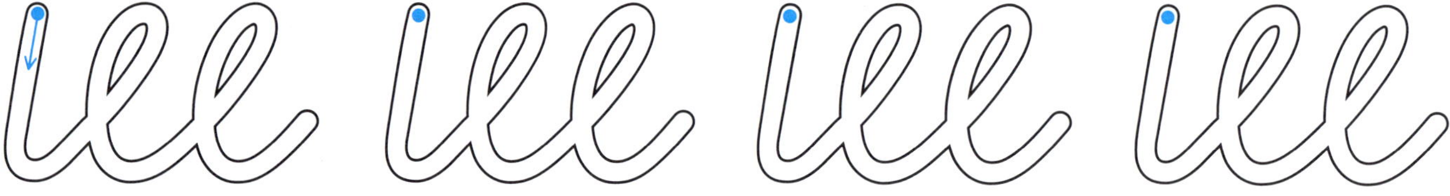

Track the letter.

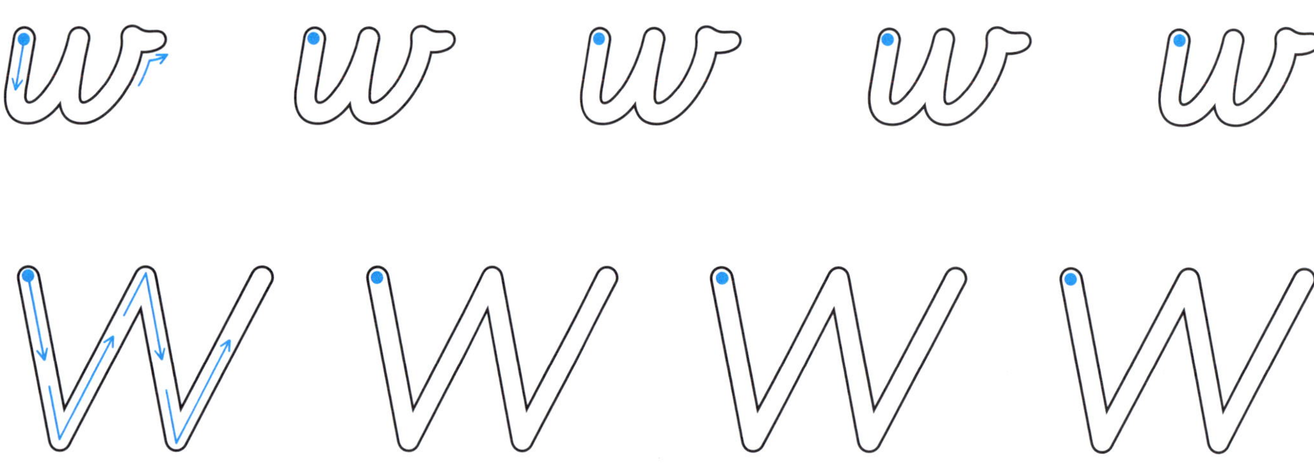

Find *w* and colour the wedge.

Trace and copy. Complete the lines.

Trace and copy.

wish wish wish

Trace and copy.

"I wish I was at home in my garage"

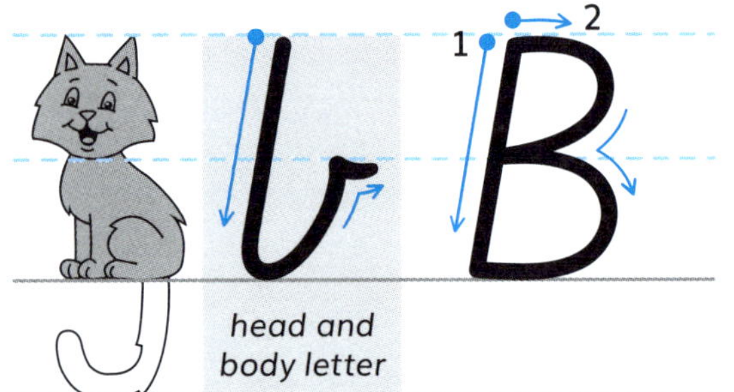

bear

Start at the blue dot. Follow the arrow.

Track the letter.

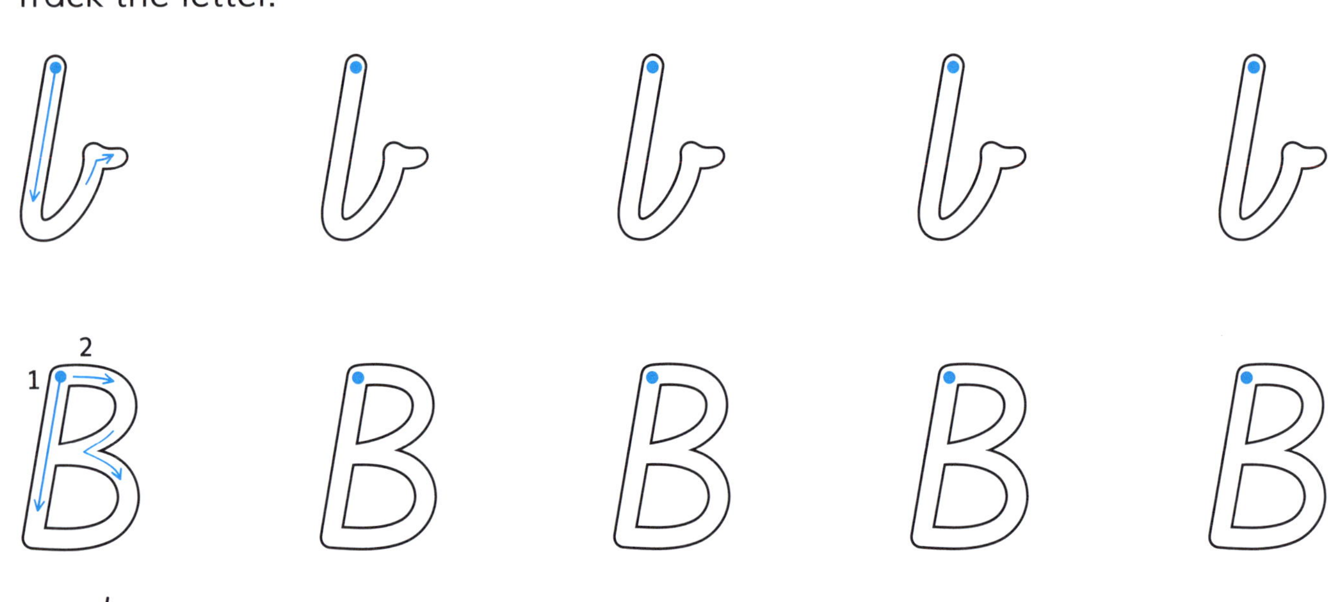

Find b.

Trace and copy. Complete the lines.

Trace and copy.

back back back

Trace and copy.

The bus was happy

to be back home.

get.ga/PMWA143

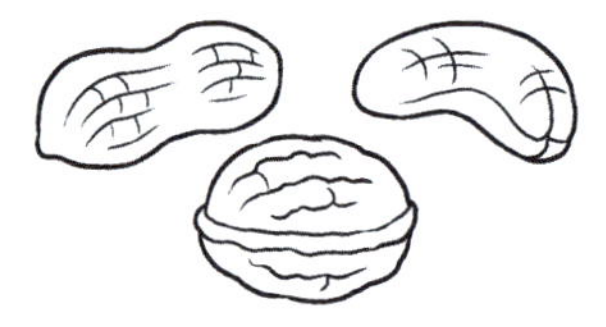

nuts

Start at the blue dot. Follow the arrow.

Track the letter.

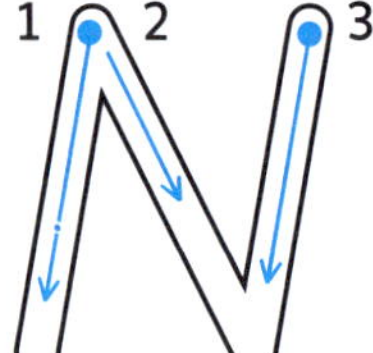

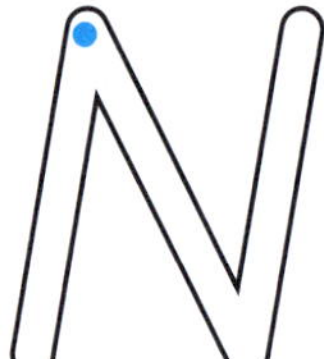

Find *n* and colour the wedge.

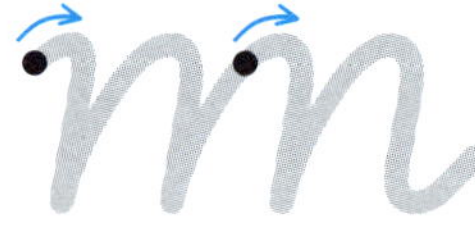

Trace and copy. Complete the lines.

Trace and copy.

near near near

Trace and copy.

The helicopter was

flying near a house.

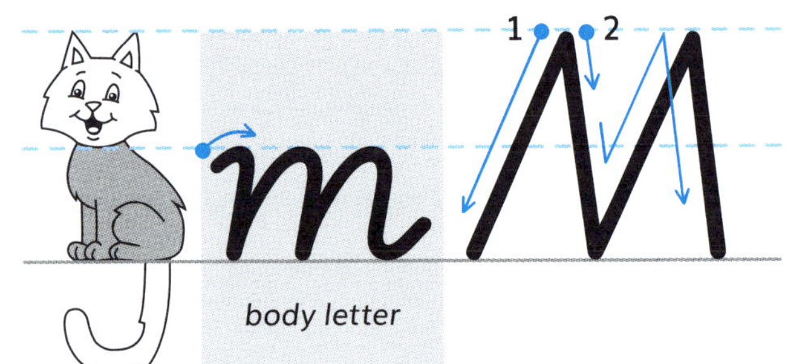

Start at the blue dot. Follow the arrow.

Track the letter.

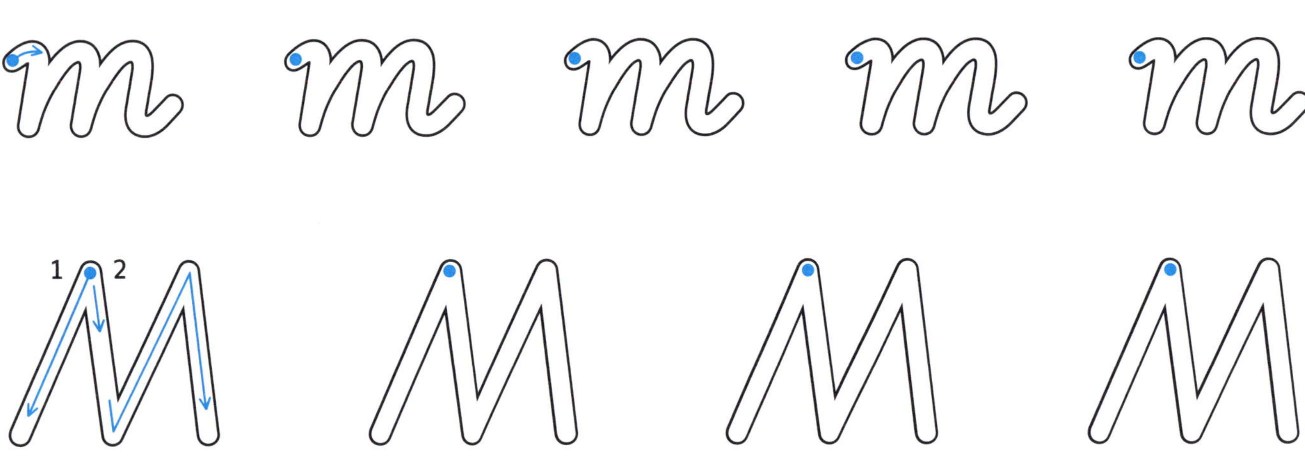

Find *m* and colour the wedges.

Trace and copy. Complete the lines.

Trace and copy.

must must must

Trace and copy.

He saw a cat. It must

be stuck, he thought.

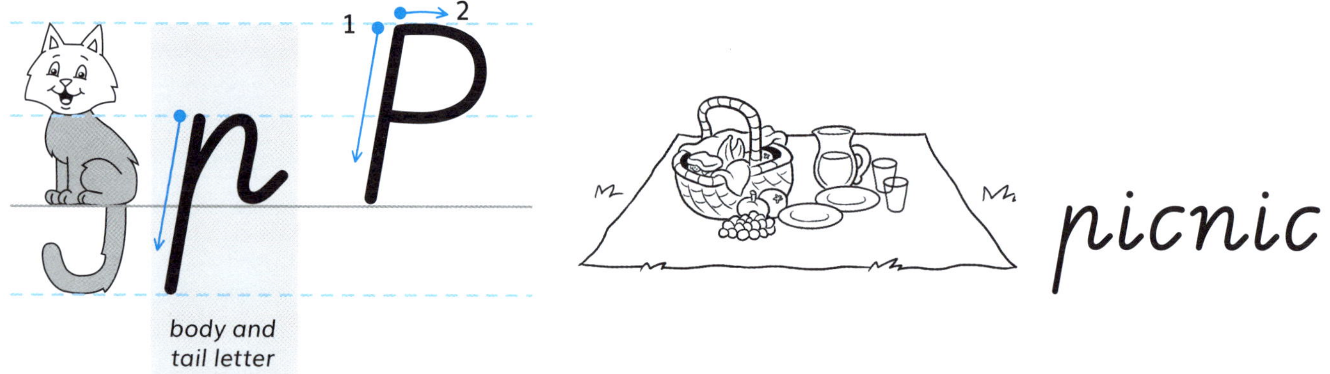

Start at the blue dot. Follow the arrow.

Track the letter.

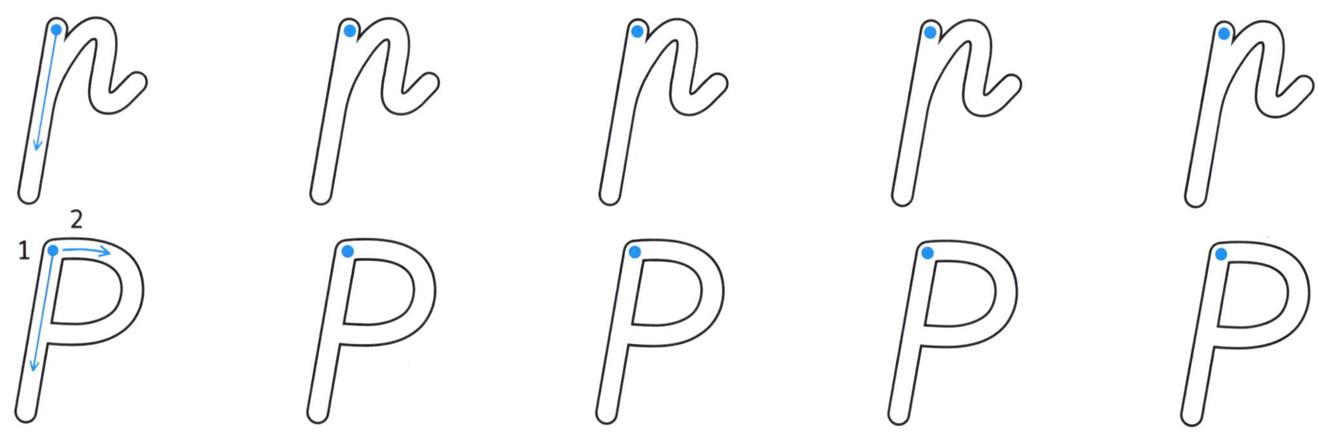

Find *p* and colour the wedge.

Trace and copy. Complete the lines.

Trace and copy.

please please please

Trace and copy.

He called the fire engine. “Please help!”

river

Start at the blue dot. Follow the arrow.

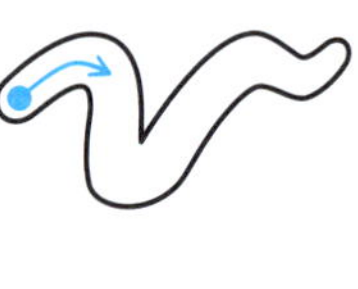

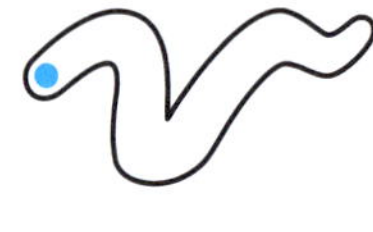

Track the letter.

Find *r* and colour the wedge.

Trace and copy. Complete the lines.

Trace and copy.

get.ga/PMWA144

Trace and copy.

"There is a little cat here on the roof."

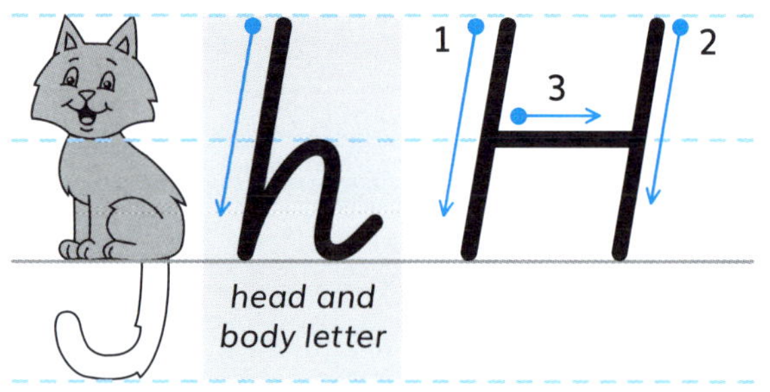

helicopter

Start at the blue dot. Follow the arrow.

Track the letter.

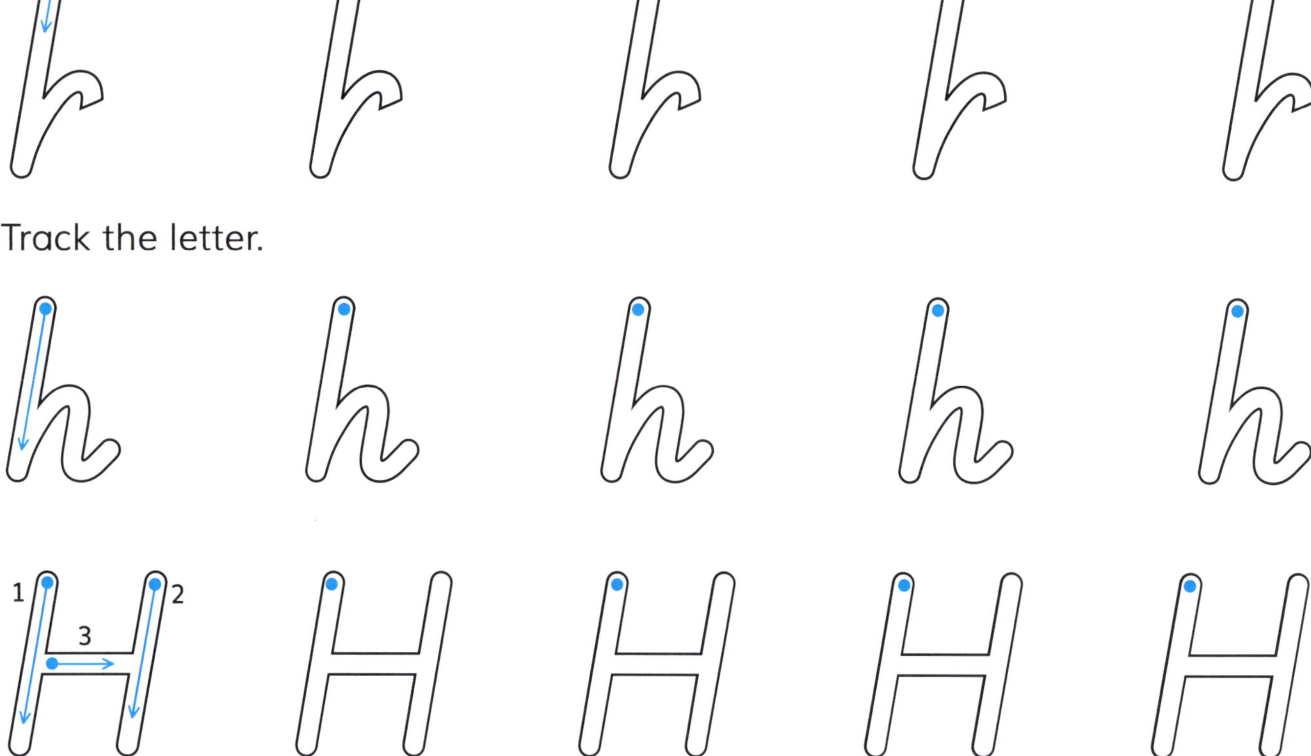

Find *h* and colour the wedge.

Trace and copy. Complete the lines.

Trace and copy.

house house house

Trace and copy.

The fire engine drove

to the house.

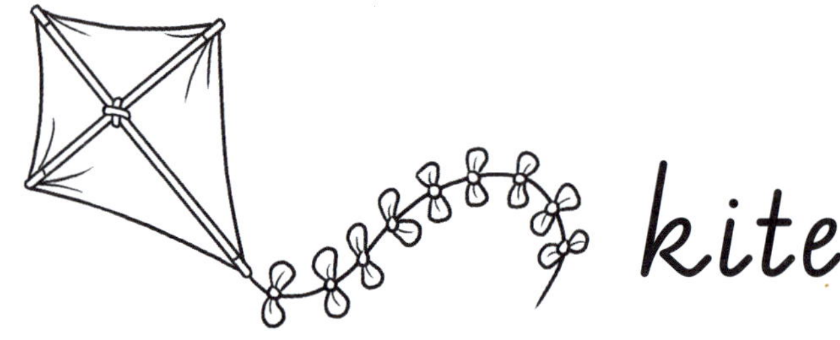

Start at the blue dot. Follow the arrow.

Track the letter.

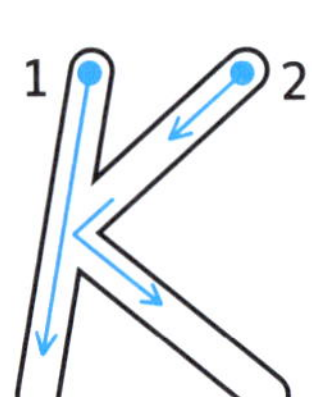

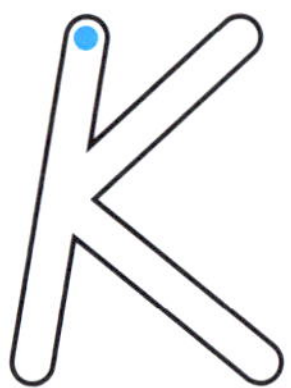   

Find *k* and colour the wedge.

 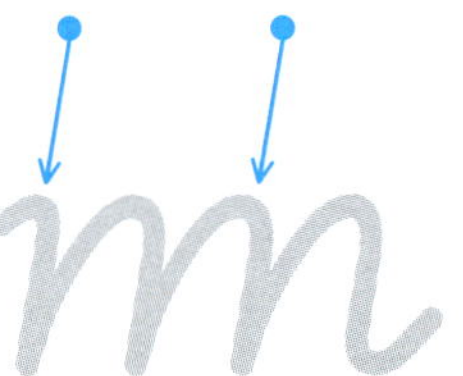 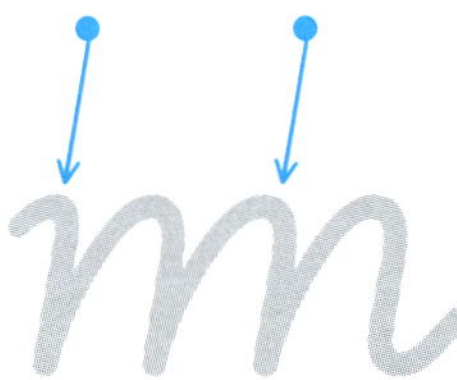 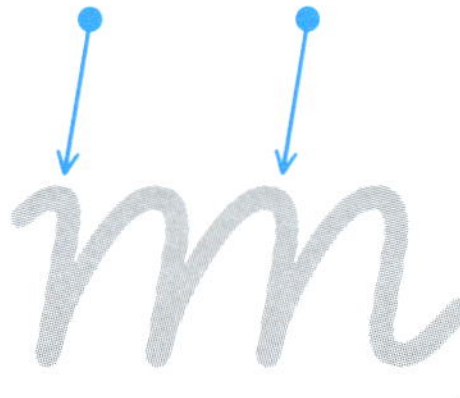

Trace and copy. Complete the lines.

Trace and copy.

keep keep keep

Trace and copy.

"Keep calm! Use my ladder to get down."

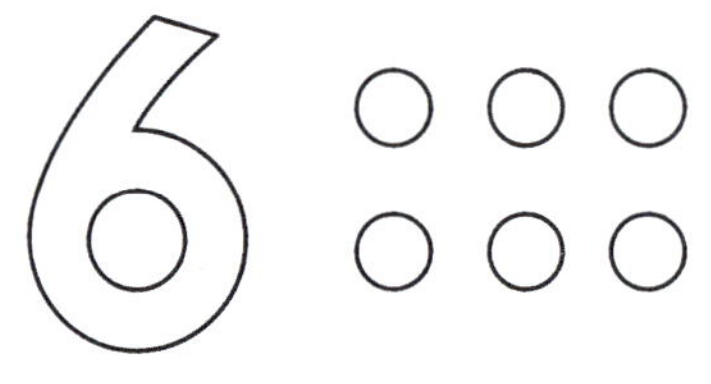

six

Start at the blue dot. Follow the arrow.

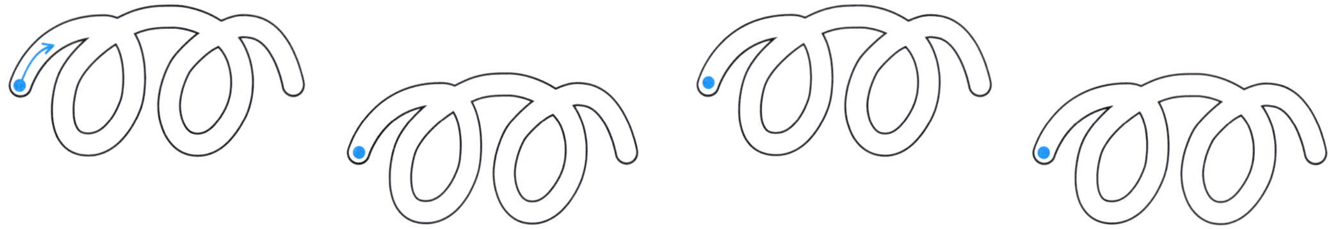

Track the letter.

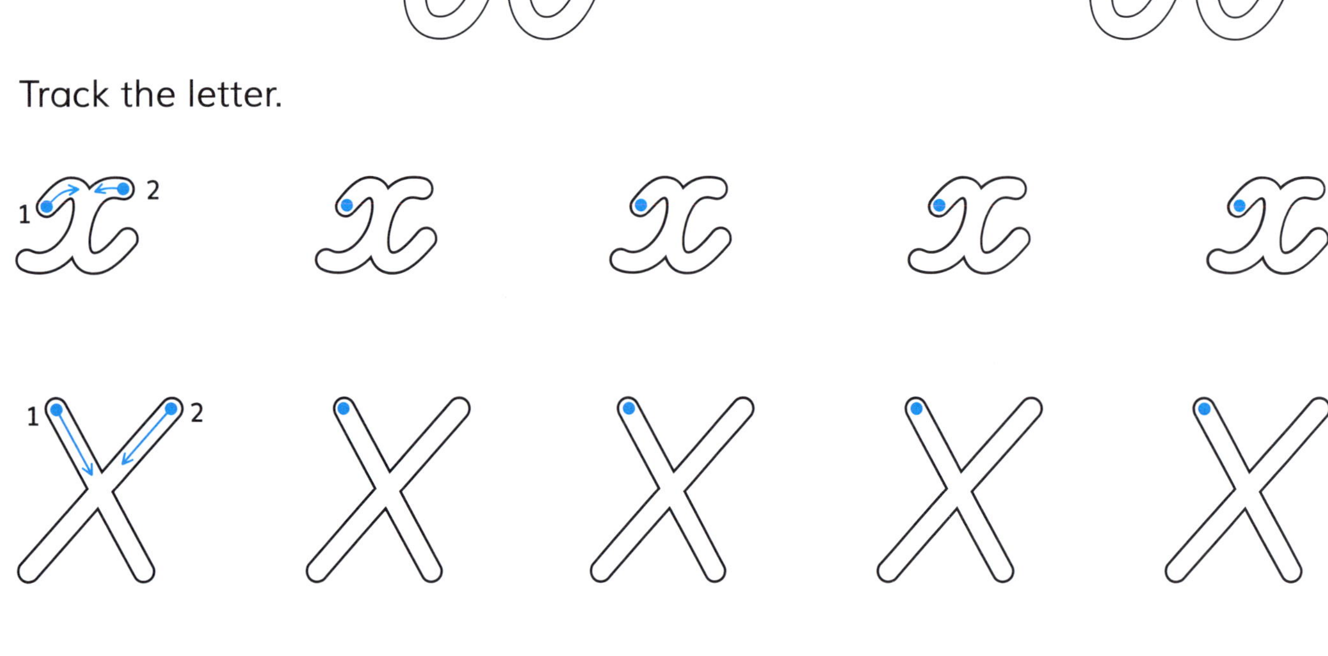

Find *x*.

Trace and copy. Complete the lines.

Trace and copy.

next next next

Trace and copy.

The cat landed next

to the fire engine.

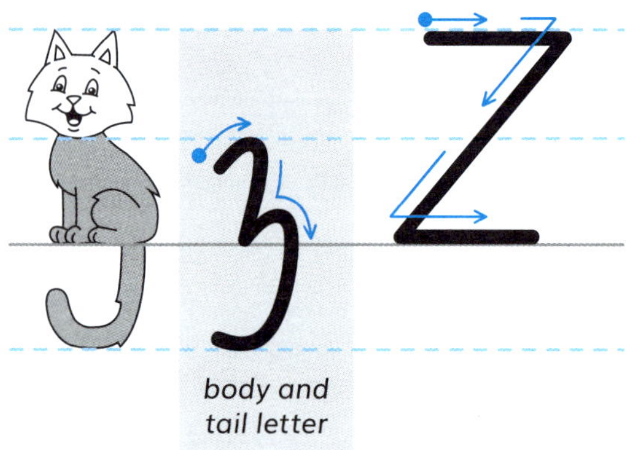

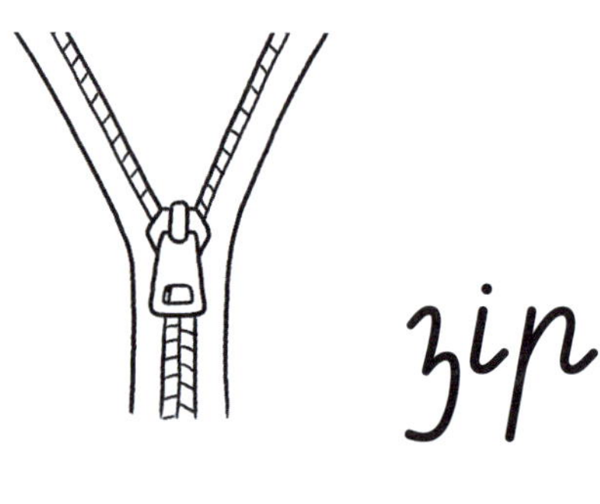

Start at the blue dot. Follow the arrow.

Track the letter.

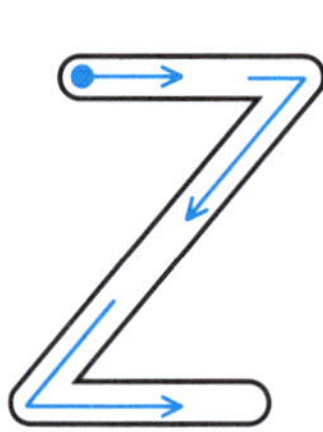    

Find z.

 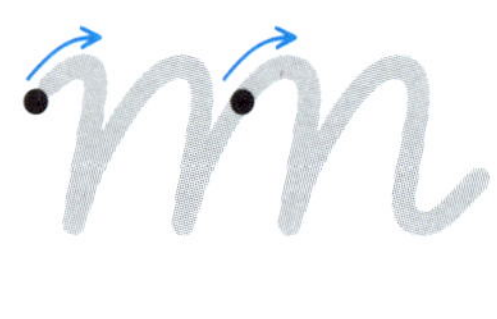  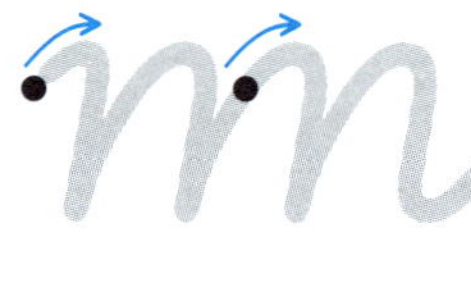

Trace and copy. Complete the lines.

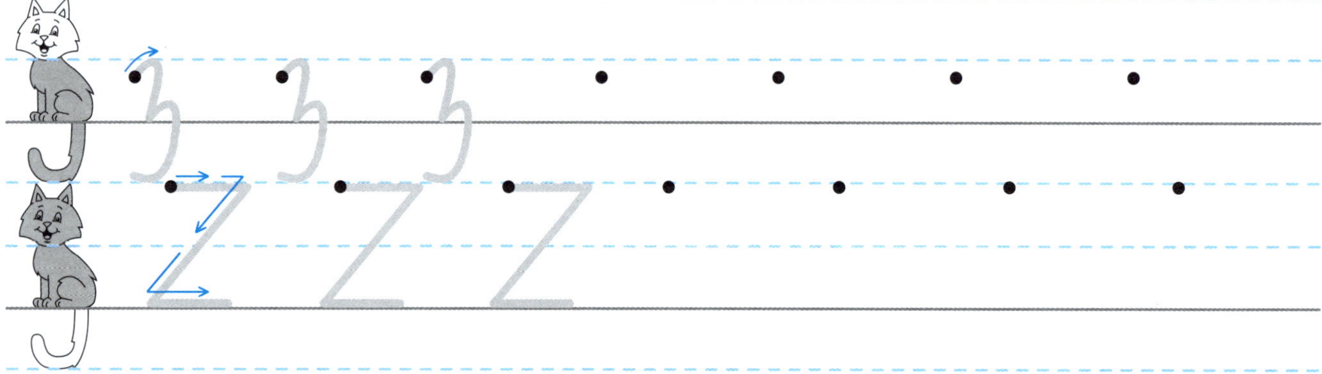

Trace and copy.

fuzzy fuzzy fuzzy

get.ga/PMWA145

Trace and copy.

Hooray! The fuzzy,

little cat is safe now.

Trace and copy.

1 one

2 two

3 three

4 four

5 five

6 six

7 seven

8 eight

9 nine

10 ten

Trace and copy.

20 twenty

30 thirty

40 forty

50 fifty

60 sixty

70 seventy

80 eighty

90 ninety

100 one

hundred

get.ga/PMWA146

Teacher observation guide

Student is: left-handed ☐ right-handed ☐

Student demonstrates correct posture, paper position and pencil grip. ☐

Student is stroking from top to bottom. ☐

Student is stroking from left to right. ☐

Student is tracking accurately. ☐

Student is tracing accurately. ☐

Student follows simple verbal rehearsal to form letters. ☐

Student forms lower-case letters with accuracy:

a	b	c	d	e	f	g	h	i	j	k	l	m	n	o	p	q	r	s	t	u	v	w	x	y	z

Student forms capital letters with accuracy:

A	B	C	D	E	F	G	H	I	J	K	L	M	N	O	P	Q	R	S	T	U	V	W	X	Y	Z

Student can write the numerals 1–100. ☐

Student uses head, body and tail character to describe the spatial properties of letters. ☐

Student can identify wedges within a letter pattern. ☐

Student is placing letters correctly within lines. ☐

Student can copy a word with accuracy. ☐

Student can copy a complete sentence with accuracy. ☐

Notes:

....

....

Date: ....